Grace
Like A Garden

by Tom Battle

Grace Like a Garden

Published by Battle Ministries
www.battleministries.com

Copyright © 2021 by Battle Ministries
461 Artesian Plaza Drive
Humble, Texas 77338-3925

ISBN 9798749506129 (Paperback-Amazon Edition)
ISBN 0-9627066-9-8 (Hardback)

What People Say About This Book

"In <u>Grace Like a Garden</u> Pastor Battle has shown with simple illustrations how to operate in the grace of God and the results it produces in our lives. As we understand the grace of God it brings freedom and liberty to help us walk out the plans and purposes that God has for our lives. As we walk out that grace we can extend it to others and bring freedom and liberty to them."

Pastor Mark Brown, Abundant Waters Fellowship,
Houston, Texas

"Tom Battle has done a phenomenal job of tucking some tremendous truths in his book. As you read it you will find blessings and encouragement on how to grow in grace and then share that blessing with others."

Pastor Oliver Stillwell, Dayspring Church,
Porter Texas

"<u>Grace Like a Garden</u> gives clear understanding of salvation for yourself and others, your need for God's presence, and His seeds that produce – multiply exponentially – and open the windows of heaven in both directions. This book provides rivers of living water through God's Word and His Holy Spirit. You will see how Jesus' light will shine through you to a lost and hurting world, as you stay yoked together with Him who is the Author and Finisher of your faith. As you press toward the prize through His growing and pruning processes, as you follow His compassion that moves you in all seasons, as you are filled with His grace, His strength will be made perfect in your weakness, and you will overcome every challenge the enemy puts in your path."

Rev. Renee Branson, Mountain Top Ministries,
Houston, Texas

"In his book <u>Grace Like a Garden</u>, Tom Battle offers vivid examples and teaching that move the reader to discover and experience the operation of God's Grace. For 30 years, I've witnessed Tom's and Schar's character, love, and daily venture of caring for the needs of others. Undoubtedly, this is reflected in Tom's exceptional ability to convey God's grace in this practical guide for Christian living."

Rev. Carl Alan Luepnitz, Eternal Love Ministries,
Saltillo and Oxaca, Mexico

"Thoughtful and timely. As I read it, my mind was challenged, my heart was warmed, my faith was strengthened and my focus was sharpened on God's grace. Praise God for giving us Jesus Christ and this book."

Pastor Jerry G. Martin, The Light of the World
Christian Fellowship, Humble, Texas

Contents

Chapter 1

Answering His Call

When I was a young boy growing up in a small town in middle Georgia during the 1950's, my parents would divide up a portion of our backyard for my two older brothers and me to plant gardens. It was a lot of fun. We looked forward to becoming little farmers as the late spring and summer approached each year. It was always exciting to smell the rich odors of the soil rising up as we turned it over with our shovels to start our gardens.

We certainly never became experts, but we did learn quite a bit about gardening by trial and error. For example, I learned that watermelons would not grow to maturity in the red soil of our backyard. I tried growing them a couple of times, and they would seem to be doing okay for a while. They would grow to the size of one of those small toy rubber footballs and then begin to shrivel. During my junior farming career, I never was able to bring a watermelon to maturity. I later heard that watermelons need a sandy type soil in order to grow well. Tomatoes, however, were a different story. I was amazed at how many luscious red tomatoes that rich red dirt would bring to beautiful maturity. I remember the first year I planted tomatoes. My harvest was so large that my mother ran out of room in the refrigerator and told me to take the rest of the tomatoes to the Piggly Wiggly grocery store. I was astonished at how much money the store manager paid me for my tomatoes, and Mother let me keep the money. Wow! That was exciting for a little kid! I experienced the thrill of entrepreneurship!

For tomatoes, I actually purchased little green tomato plants at the feed store. After setting out the young plants, I would carefully tie them to wooden stakes with old strips of soft fabric. It was important to persistently inspect, adjust, and add strips of cloth as the plants grew in order to keep the young tomatoes off the ground. For other crops, I purchased seed packets which contained instructions on the best time for planting and some other basic information regarding how far apart to plant the seeds, watering requirements, etc. Keeping grass and weeds out of my garden was very important, especially when the plants were young. The most effective way to combat grass and weeds was to pull them out by their roots with my hands rather than to use a hoe. Watering was crucial, especially during droughts. It was important to be consistent. Skipping days and then trying to play catch-up did not make for a healthy garden.

Looking back on my life, it has been much like a garden. I did not enter into a personal relationship with the Lord Jesus until I was 38 years of age. The garden of my life was overrun with weeds and whatever grew on its own accord. Whatever wild seeds blew my way usually found a place to germinate in the soil of my life. At an early age I experienced immense success in the oil industry, but the weeds of alcoholism and substance abuse began to choke out everything else. I had become a multimillionaire by the age of thirty, but the garden of my life was completely overrun by the weeds of addictions by the age of thirty-eight. My business empire was in shambles as the oil-bust of the 1980s hit Houston, Texas. But on February 24, 1985, I turned the garden of my life over to Jesus Christ, the great farmer of souls. He immediately ripped the weeds of addiction out of the garden of my life. He removed me from the oil industry and placed me in ministry. One could say that He changed out the topsoil of my garden. I experienced God's amazing grace, and it continues in my life. Grace to me is like a garden.

Mankind began in the Garden of Eden; and though Adam and Eve were cast out because of sin, God has made the paradise of grace available to all of us through His Son Jesus Christ. When a person accepts Jesus as his or her personal Lord and Savior, paradise takes up residence in that person's heart. Jesus becomes the gardener of the believer's heart and life.

Perhaps one of the saddest verses in the Bible is found in Genesis chapter 3, verse 9: *Then the LORD God called to Adam and said to him, "Where are you?"* Because of their sin of eating the forbidden fruit, Adam and Eve had hidden themselves from God when they heard Him walking in the Garden of Eden. I believe that the main reason God created mankind was to have fellowship with us. That day in the garden, God was looking forward to visiting with His creation which He had made in His own image. However, Adam and Eve were hiding. They were ashamed of their nakedness because they knew, that by their disobedience, they had tarnished the image in which God had created them. After having made a feeble attempt to cover themselves with clothes made from fig leaves, they decided to hide among the trees in the garden. But no one can really hide from God.

As a result of their sin, they were cast out of the garden, but not before God clothed them with tunics made from animal hides. The making of the tunics involved the killing and shedding of the blood of innocent animals. This was the first of many animal sacrifices that were to be recorded in the Bible. These sacrifices gave mankind hope. They pointed to a

Redeemer, a Messiah, a sinless Savior who would eventually allow His precious blood to be poured out on a cross at Calvary in order to satisfy God's judgment for all of our sins.

God, in His mercy, banned Adam and Eve from the Garden of Eden because He did not want them to eat of its tree of life. Had they eaten of that tree in their sinful state, they would have been locked into their sins forever, and all hope for mankind would have been lost. God in His great wisdom and love provided another tree of life for humanity, the cross of Christ. It was on this tree that Jesus not only provided eternal life for us; He also took away all of our sins. It was on the tree at Calvary that Jesus satisfied God's righteous judgment for our sins. He paid the price with His precious blood to set us free from our sins and to give us an eternal relationship with His Father.

This tree of life, the cross of Christ, is available to everyone. No one is banned from coming to the cross of Christ, but we must come to it on the merits of Jesus. When we attempt to come to the cross on our own merits, we are like Adam and Eve trying to clothe themselves with fig leaves. Paul put it this way: *"For all have sinned and fall short of the glory of God"* (Romans 3:23). When we try to cover our sins through our own works (even though our works might be good and even appear religious) we always come up short.

God is calling out to everyone, "Where are you?" One can only answer the call by turning to Jesus and accepting the clothes of righteousness that He paid for on His cross with His blood. The Bible uses the word "repentance" to describe this turn to God. It is a word that originated with nomadic people, and it meant to turn toward home. It implies that one has been going in the wrong direction with his or her life and is deciding to make the turn to God which is only available through Jesus. When a person repents, he or she, in humility acknowledges the error of his or her way and turns to the cross of Jesus for forgiveness and new life. Peter confirmed that the Lord is calling everyone to repentance in 2 Peter 3:9: *"The Lord is not slack concerning His promise, as some count slackness, but is long suffering toward us, not willing that any should perish but that all should come to repentance."*

In Acts chapter 4, Peter and John, even though they had been imprisoned for healing a lame man in the name of Jesus, refused to adhere to the Sanhedrin's demand that they not minister in His name. Peter, in reference to Jesus, said, *"Nor is there salvation in any other, for there is no other name under heaven given among men by which we must be saved"* (Acts 4:12).

There is only one tree of life available to mankind. It is the cross of Christ. Jesus declared to His disciple Thomas (whose name means "seeker of truth") that He is the only way in John 14:6: *Jesus said to him, "I am the way, the truth, and the life. No one comes to the Father except through Me."*

Yes, God is calling to everyone, "Where are you?" No one can answer the call for us. Each person has to respond for himself. Jesus has done the hard part by suffering and dying for our sins. Jesus is the only person who ever walked this planet without sin. The Apostle Peter said this about Jesus in 1 Peter 2:22-24*: Who committed no sin, nor was deceit found in His mouth; who, when He was reviled, did not revile in return; when He suffered, He did not threaten, but committed Himself to Him who judges righteously; who Himself bore our sins in His own body on the tree, that we, having died to sins, might live for righteousness – by whose stripes you were healed.*

The Apostle Paul backs this up with his statement about Jesus in 2 Corinthians 5:21: *For He made Him who knew no sin to be sin for us, that we might become the righteousness of God in Him.* Jesus is the only one qualified to pay the price for our sins. He did this when He died on the cross at Calvary. The last words spoken by Jesus from the cross just before He died, as recorded by John, were, *"It is finished"* (from John 19:30). Archaeological finds from that period show these same words on papyrus receipts for "paid in full." When Jesus said, "It is finished," He was, in effect, saying that the price for our salvation has been paid in full by His death on the tree at Calvary. The works of Jesus on that tree have become our tree of life. The cross is open to every person. No one, no matter how evil he or she might be, is over a decision away from forgiveness and a new life in Christ. All God requires is that decision to repent, to turn away from the way of the world and to embrace Jesus Christ as one's personal Lord and Savior.

Jesus was crucified between two thieves that day at Calvary. One of the thieves ridiculed Jesus, but the other thief acknowledged his own sins in an attitude of repentance. He turned to Jesus, calling Him Lord and asking Him to remember him in His coming kingdom. The response of Jesus to the repentant thief is given in Luke chapter 23, verse 43: *And Jesus said to him, "Assuredly, I say to you, today you will be with Me in Paradise."* There was nothing the repentant thief could do to earn his salvation. He was nailed to a cross. The only thing he did was to make a decision to acknowledge Jesus as Lord and to commit his future and his life to Him. He found paradise on a cross. In 2005, I was inspired to write the lyrics to a song about the repentant thief's experience:

Paradise

Verse 1

Many mocked the King upon the cross
Including another thief who was lost
But this one confessed his sin
And he asked the Lord to remember him
In Paradise

Verse 2

He rebuked the other one from his cross
Saying to the thief who was lost
This Man Jesus is innocent
And he asked the Lord to remember him
In Paradise

Chorus

Today you will be with Me in Paradise
Those were the sweetest words he'd heard in all his life
Paradise ….. who would have thought
That this is the way to Paradise
Who would have thought
That this is the King of Paradise[1]

When we take our lives to the cross of Christ in repentance and surrender to Him as Lord, we find paradise. Jesus gives us a new life and brings paradise to our hearts. Our lives become the garden of the Lord when we make that decision of surrender to Him. Jesus becomes the great gardener of our lives.

The tomb where Jesus was buried was donated by Joseph of Arimathea and was actually located in a garden near where He was crucified. John 19:41-42 reads, *"Now in the place where He was crucified there was a garden, and in the garden a new tomb in which no one had yet been laid. So there they laid Je-*

sus, because of the Jews' Preparation Day, for the tomb was nearby."

It's very interesting that Mary Magdalene supposed the risen Jesus to be the gardener when He appeared to her at the garden tomb site. This is documented in the verses below:

John 20:11-16: *But Mary stood outside by the tomb weeping, and as she wept she stooped down and looked into the tomb. And she saw two angels in white sitting, one at the head and the other at the feet, where the body of Jesus had lain. Then they said to her, "Woman why are you weeping?"*

She said to them, "Because they have taken away my Lord, and I do not know where they have laid Him."

Now when she had said this, she turned around and saw Jesus standing there, and did not know that it was Jesus. Jesus said to her, "Woman, why are you weeping? Whom are you seeking?"

She, supposing Him to be the gardener, said to Him, "Sir, if You have carried Him away, tell me where You have laid Him, and I will take Him away."

Jesus said to her, "Mary!"

She turned and said to Him, "Rabboni" (which is to say, Teacher).

Again, Mary's first impression of the risen Jesus was that He was the gardener! When we accept Him as our personal Lord and Savior, He begins His gardening in our hearts and lives. He calls out to us and, like Mary, we know His voice. He is always there loving us, teaching us, nourishing us, watering us, weeding us, pruning us, propping us up, and giving us the fruit of harvest. He knows each one of us individually by name and calls out to us just as He did to Mary that day at the garden tomb site. Each one of us is so important to Him that He would have gone to the cross if there were only one of us. He loves everyone that much! All of us are individually in His thoughts and loving care every moment of every day. He can do this because of His omnipresence (present everywhere at the same time) and omniscience (the state of knowing everything), which He has through the Holy Spirit. If you have not turned the garden of your life over to the Lord Jesus, you are only a decision away from doing so. You can answer His call on your life by saying the following prayer of decision with sincerity of heart.

Lord Jesus, I repent for the way I have been living by turning to You with my whole heart for forgiveness, salvation, and a new beginning. I accept You now and forever as my personal Lord and Savior. Thank You for bringing paradise to my heart and becoming the gardener of my life. In Your name, the name of Jesus, amen.

Chapter 2

Grace for Grace

There are several good definitions for the word *grace*. I really like the acronym:

G — God's
R — Riches
A — At
C — Christ's
E — Expense

Another simple and easy to remember definition that we often hear is "unmerited favor." *Webster's* first definition for *grace* is "unmerited divine assistance given man for his regeneration or sanctification."[2]

The New Testament was originally written in the Greek language. *Strong's* defines *charis* (the Greek word for grace) as "the divine influence upon the heart, and its reflection in the life."[3] This definition helps us to understand what John meant when he wrote, *"And of His fullness we have all received, and grace for grace"* (John 1:16). Real grace should produce more grace. Salvation is not an end but a beginning. When we accept Jesus Christ as our Lord and Savior, our hearts and lives become His garden. Like any good gardener, He comes bearing seed. Every seed contains an embryo of the plant it will produce, and every plant produces fruit that contains more seed. "Grace for grace" clearly implies "grace like a garden!"

All of us, before turning to Jesus, allowed the wrong kind of seeds to be planted in the gardens of our lives. As I mentioned earlier, my life before accepting Christ had become a tangled mess of weeds and thorns. Selfishness, pride, lust, and confusion seemed to be in charge most of the time. I needed to turn the farm of my heart over to someone who knew what he was doing, and that is exactly what happened when I surrendered to Jesus. After all these years, the divine influence of His grace continues to be reflected in the garden of my life, and I give Him all the glory!

John in the first chapter of his Gospel identifies Jesus as the Word: *In the beginning was the Word, and the Word was with God, and the Word was God. He was in the beginning with God. All things were made through Him, and without Him nothing was made that was made. In Him was life, and the life was the light of men* (vv. 1-3). *And the Word became flesh and dwelt among us, and we beheld His glory, the glory as of the only begotten of the Father, full of grace and truth* (v.14). Jesus has always been the Word. He was the Word with the Father before time began, and He was the Word when He was born of the Virgin Mary. He is the resurrected Word that lives in our hearts today through the Holy Spirit who raised Him from the dead!

Every time we read God's written word, the Bible, we are allowing Jesus, the gardener of our lives, to plant His seed in our hearts. In Galatians 3:19 Paul refers to Jesus as *"the Seed."* Also, very early in the Bible, God refers to the coming Messiah, the Promised One, as the Seed of the woman in Genesis 3:15, and from there it continues to be used as a messianic term throughout the Bible (see Numbers 24:7 and Isaiah 53:10). Paul also verifies this in Galatians 3:16: *Now to Abraham and his Seed were the promises made. He does not say, "And to seeds," as of many, but as of one, "And to Your Seed," who is Christ.*

Jesus is the Word, and He is the Seed. As we spiritually digest God's word, Jesus is planting His seed in the gardens of our hearts. Again, every seed contains an embryo of the plant it will produce, and every plant produces fruit that contains more seed. The Seed of Christ, the Word of God, is the source of our new life in Him, as 1 Peter 1:23 confirms: *having been born again, not of corruptible seed but incorruptible, through the word of God which lives and abides forever.* Romans 8:29 tells those of us who have answered His call that we are being *"conformed to the image of His Son."* It all begins with the new birth, but it doesn't end there. As we allow this wonderful gardener Jesus to plant the seed of His word in the soil of our hearts and souls, we become more and more like Him. Grace, that divine influence upon our hearts and lives, begins to multiply and transform us more and more into the image of Jesus. As John the Baptist said in reference to Jesus, *"He must increase, but I must decrease"* (John 3:30).

My wife Schar surrendered her life to Jesus about two years before my salvation experience. Because of the changes I saw in her life, I bought a Bible and started reading it. I did not realize it until later, but every time I opened that Bible, I was planting the incorruptible seed of the Word of God in my heart and soul. Finally, I made that decision to surrender all to Jesus, and all those seeds that had been germinating in my inner man sprang to life. I became a new creation in Christ. As Paul put it in 2 Corinthians 5:17: *Therefore if anyone is in Christ, he is a new creation; old things have passed away; behold, all things have become new.*

Immediately upon experiencing God's grace in my life, I wanted to tell others and share His wonderful grace with them. I have been doing this for the last thirty-six years, and I don't intend to stop! The ministry God has given me has truly been one of "grace for grace." God has called all of us to be witnesses unto Jesus. The Bible refers to this as the ministry of reconciliation in 2 Corinthians 5:18-19: *Now all things are of God, who has reconciled us to Himself through Jesus Christ, and has given us the ministry of reconciliation, that is that God was in Christ reconciling the world to Himself, not imputing their trespasses to them, and has committed to us the word of reconciliation.* Paul did not say, "committed to me." He said, "committed to us." He meant that this ministry of leading others into relationship with God through Jesus Christ belongs to all believers. God is a farmer. He wants to see the Seed of His Son Jesus reproduced throughout humanity. Sharing the seeds of the Scriptures and the seeds of our personal testimonies with others is a great way of planting the Seed, Jesus Christ, in their hearts.

We've all heard people say, "I'm a Christian, but I consider my faith a private matter. I don't share my personal beliefs with others." That kind of attitude is not biblical. For example, Proverbs 11:30 states, *"The fruit of the righteous is a tree of life, and he who wins souls is wise."* Jesus said, *"Preach on the housetops"* (Matthew 10:27). I believe Jesus was speaking to all of us when He said, *"You are the light of the world. A city that is set on a hill cannot be hidden. Nor do they light a lamp and put it under a basket, but on a lampstand, and it gives light to all who are in the house. Let your light so shine before men, that they may see your good works and glorify your Father in heaven"* (Matthew 5:14-16). The lamp produced an open flame. To put it under a wooden basket would cause a destructive fire in the home. When we keep quiet about our faith, we are taking part in the eternal fires of suffering for unreached souls! The words that we speak and the lives that we lead are seeds from the gardens of our hearts and should reflect the divine influence (grace) in us. Again, it is "grace for grace."

Roy B. Zuck in The Speaker's Quote Book gives the following illustration under the heading *"Children Must be Taught While They are Young"*:

The English poet Samuel Coleridge talked with a man who did not believe that children should be given any religious instruction at all. The man claimed that the child's mind should not be prejudiced in any direction, and when he became older he should be permitted to choose his religious opinions for himself. Coleridge said nothing; but after a while he asked his visitor if he would like to see his garden, where only weeds were growing. The man looked at Coleridge in surprise, and said, "Why this is not a garden! There is nothing but weeds here!"

"Well, you see," answered Coleridge, "I did not wish to infringe upon the liberty of the garden in any way. I was just giving the garden a chance to express itself and to choose its own production." [4]

The truth, as Samuel Coleridge so aptly pointed out to his visitor, is that if we don't plant seeds of truth and grace in the gardens of our children's lives, the same enemy who deceived Adam and Eve in the Garden of Eden will sow the seeds of his weeds of deception in the unplanted soil of their hearts and minds. Grace does carry a responsibility with it. It is "grace for grace."

We are saved by grace through faith as Ephesians 2:8-9 confirms: *For by grace you have been saved through faith, and that not of yourselves; it is the gift of God, not of works, lest anyone should boast.* But the scripture does not end there, and neither does grace. The next verse goes on to say, *"For we*

are His workmanship, created in Christ Jesus for good works,
which God prepared beforehand that we should walk in them"
(verse 10). God brought His paradise to our hearts so that we
could sow its seeds into the lives of others. It truly is "grace
for grace!" Good works that God prepared beforehand for our
lives spring forth from the merits of Jesus rather than our own
and are expressions of His grace growing in our hearts. These
Spirit-led works are different from legalistic works. Legalistic
works are man trying to earn God's favor through efforts that
might appear to be good or religious. The person who is con-
trolled by legalism tries to buy God's favor with his works,
but the Christian who understands his salvation knows that the
works of Jesus at Calvary have already secured God's favor
for him. The realization that our works are seeds rather than
payments can help us to avoid the error of religious legalism.

Years ago, the slogan WWJD became popular among Christians. It is a good saying and means:

W — What
W — Would
J — Jesus
D — Do

This is a good question to ask oneself at crossroads of decision, but I believe there is another acronym that is also very
good:

W — What
I — Is
J — Jesus
D — Doing

We need to realize that the great gardener, Jesus, is already
at work in our situations. Many times, the decision we need

to make is merely to embrace what He is already doing. As Proverbs 3:5-6 puts it: *"Trust in the LORD with all your heart, and lean not on your own understanding; in all your ways acknowledge Him, and He shall direct your paths."* The Hebrew word used here for "acknowledge" is *yada*. According to *Strong's*, *yada* can mean to "be aware" or to "discern."[5] Our objective should not be to move God but rather to move with God. Religious legalism carries the thought that one can buy his way with God; whereas, grace carries the thought of flowing with God.

As we contemplate our lives, we need to ask ourselves, "What is that great gardener Jesus doing in this situation? Is He pulling out weeds and thorns that have been choking my productivity? Is He breaking up soil, plowing, and planting new seeds? Is He harvesting fruit and accompanying seeds from my garden to use in sowing into the lives of others? WIJD – what is Jesus doing?"

Paul told the Corinthian believers that they were living epistles or letters in 2 Corinthians 3:3: *Clearly you are an epistle of Christ, ministered by us, written not with ink but by the Spirit of the living God, not on tablets of stone but on tablets of flesh, that is, of the heart.* As believers, we need to be aware that others are observing our hearts and lives. To some people, our lives may be the only Bible that they ever read! With others, they might be drawn to God's written word as they see its reality being displayed in our lives. When my wife began to love me the way Jesus loves, I became determined to find out what had happened to her. I observed her going to church and reading the Bible regularly, so my search led me to the Bible. Schar's becoming an *epistle of Christ* made me hungry for God's Word, which eventually led to my total surrender to Jesus with my life.

Since my surrender to Jesus, nearly every day has started by my opening the Bible and allowing the gardener of my life to plant the seed of His word in the soil of my inner man. As His seed has produced seed bearing fruit, I have been able to sow into the lives of others. Paul spoke of this fruit in Galatians 5:22-23: *But the fruit of the Spirit is love, joy, peace, longsuffering, kindness, goodness, faithfulness, gentleness, self-control. Against such there is no law.* This fruit is first described as love, and all of its other characteristics are cousins of love. God the Father is love. Jesus is love. The Holy Spirit is love. The fruit of the Spirit contains the seed of love. When others partake of the fruit that the garden of the believer's life produces, they are receiving spiritual seed that contains an embryo of love and grace. So, we see that not only are our words seeds, but so are our actions and overall attitudes. I am convinced that if we will allow the Holy Spirit to produce His fruit in the gardens of our lives, that same Spirit will bring hungry hearts to us.

Not only does the fruit of the Spirit contain seed, the flowers of our gardens bear seeds, ready to be spread by the wind of the Holy Spirit. As we yield to the Spirit and to the Word, our gardens bloom with seed bearing flowers that are attractive to lost and hurting humanity. This is exciting because the wind of the Holy Spirit can take the seeds from our gardens to places we never even imagined! Not only that, the blooms in your garden may be pollinating paradise in other believers' hearts, as you yield to the wind of God's grace and love! Our mission truly is "grace for grace!"

When I see or smell a beautiful flower, I am reminded of our Creator's love for us. He obviously made them lovely and fragrant for our enjoyment. I try to give my wife flowers every week as an expression of my love for her. God gave mankind flowers because of His love for us. One excellent way to inspect life's garden is to ask oneself, "Am I bearing and giving off the taste, the fragrance, and the beauty of love?"

Paul gives a great description of love in 1 Corinthians 13:4-8a: *Love suffers long and is kind; love does not envy; love does not parade itself, is not puffed up; does not behave rudely, does not seek its own, is not provoked, thinks no evil; does not rejoice in iniquity, but rejoices in the truth; bears all things, believes all things, hopes all things, endures all things. Love never fails.* These verses are an excellent way to examine the fragrance of the gardens of our lives. As we compare our gardens to these verses, we are conducting a spiritual sniff test.

When I surrendered my heart to Jesus on February 24, 1985, I was totally amazed. I stood there suddenly free from my addictions, which I knew had been killing me. I had tried to free myself many times through "will power," but my fleshly efforts always failed. However, upon accepting Jesus as my personal Lord and Savior, I felt the addictions leave as the Spirit of Christ moved into my heart. I was so appreciative. I remember asking God, "What can I do for you?" The Lord responded by blowing a directive across my spirit to go out and show others the same love that He had shown me. It was really His way of telling me that it's "grace for grace" as the Scripture says (John 1:16).

If you would like to make a "grace for grace" commitment, I offer the following prayer and confession:

Father God, I come to You in the name of your Son Jesus asking for Your grace to produce the fruit of Your Spirit in the garden of my heart and life. As I yield the soil of my inner man to Your Spirit and to Your Word, I pray that the fragrance of my life's garden will be attractive to all those around me, drawing them closer to You. I pray that over my lifetime, the wind of Your Spirit will sow the Seed of Christ from my heart to the hearts of many others. May my life truly be one of grace for grace! Amen.

20

Chapter 3

The Throne of Grace

Aren't you glad that the fruit of the Spirit is not hatred, outbursts of wrath, contentions, envy, unfaithfulness, murder, and the like? These types of attitudes and actions are actually referred to as works of the flesh in Galatians 5:19-21: *Now the works of the flesh are evident, which are*: *adultery, fornication, uncleanness, lewdness, idolatry, sorcery, hatred, contentions, jealousies, outbursts of wrath, selfish ambitions, dissensions, heresies, envy, murders, drunkenness, revelries, and the like; of which I tell you beforehand, just as I also told you in time past, that those who practice such things will not inherit the kingdom of God.* The Greek word for *flesh* is "sarx." According to *Strong's*, the word can refer to our physical bodies; or, as used in the above verses, it is a reference to the human nature with its moral and physical frailties.[6] In short, as used here, it means the weakness of one's humanity. When a Christian practices or continually engages in the works of the flesh, he is yielding the soil of his inner man to the wrong kinds of seeds. He is sowing to the flesh rather than to the spirit and is denying himself the inheritance that is rightfully his as a child of God.

The same enemy that deceived Adam and Eve in the Garden of Eden is still around today, and he brings with him seeds of temptation that are contrary to the Word of God. Paul got right to the point when he wrote: *"Do not be deceived, God is not mocked; for whatever a man sows, that he will also reap. For he who sows to his flesh will of the flesh reap corruption, but he who sows to the Spirit will of the Spirit reap everlasting life"* (Galatians 6:7-8).

John the Baptist, in pointing the people to Jesus, said, *"He who believes in the Son has everlasting life"* (John3:36a). According to Jesus Himself in John 5:24, those of us who have entrusted our lives to Him already have everlasting life: *"Most assuredly, I say to you, he who hears My word and believes in Him who sent Me has everlasting life, and shall not come into judgment, but has passed from death into life."* As believers, we already have everlasting life.

The question is, "Are we reaping the harvest that should be produced by the everlasting life within us?" Or to put it another way, "Are we experiencing our full inheritance as children of God?" If we look around us and see the gardens of our lives overrun with weeds and thorns, it means that we have allowed the same enemy who tricked Adam and Eve to deceive us. If we see the works of the flesh being exhibited in our lives instead of the fruit of the Spirit, it means we have sown to the flesh rather than to the Spirit. However, God loves us, and He has provided a place to us go for elimination of weeds and briers. It is called the throne of grace (Hebrews 4:16). The word *throne* implies the existence of a kingdom.

When Jesus was asked a question about the kingdom of God, He answered in part, *"the kingdom of God is within you"* (Luke 17:21). When a person truly surrenders his heart to the Lord Jesus, He takes up residence in that person's heart. Jesus brings His kingdom to the earth one heart and soul at a time. The Father of Jesus becomes our Father, and we become *"joint heirs of God with Christ"* (Romans 8:17) when we make a now and forever decision to accept Jesus Christ as our personal Lord and Savior. The paradise that Jesus brings to our hearts is also a kingdom. The gardener of our hearts and lives is also a king. Paradise thrives when we yield to the king and open the soil of our hearts to His Spirit and Word. Our inheritance includes the fruit of the Spirit and all the wonderful promises of God willed to us in the Holy Scriptures by the death, burial, and resurrection of Jesus!

Our king is also our high priest, and the throne from which He reigns in our hearts is a place of grace and mercy. It is there that we go for the uprooting and removal of the weeds and briers, otherwise known as the works of the flesh.

Hebrews 4:15-16: *For we do not have a High Priest who cannot sympathize with our weaknesses, but was in all points tempted as we are, yet without sin. Let us therefore come boldly to the throne of grace, that we may obtain mercy and find grace to help in time of need.*

This "throne of grace" is a place of sympathy and understanding rather than judgment and condemnation. Jesus loves us with the greatest love ever known to mankind. In talking of His approaching crucifixion, He said, *"Greater love has no one than this, than to lay down one's life for his friends"* (John 15:13). Jesus called all of us His friends when He went to the cross for us.

All of us need to spend time in the throne room of grace that the king, high priest, and gardener of our lives has set up within us. It's like a beautiful gazebo in the center of our hearts. Jesus is always there to listen as we confess and ask forgiveness for allowing the enemy to sow his seeds into our lives. He understands and is always ready to forgive, to uproot, and to cleanse. *"If we confess our sins, He is faithful and just to forgive us our sins and to cleanse us from all unrighteousness"* (1 John 1:9). "Unrighteousness" here refers to behavior that is not right in the eyes of God.

The words that Isaiah spoke to Israel in Isaiah 1:18 also speak to us today: *"Come now, and let us reason together,"* *says the LORD, "Though your sins are like scarlet, they shall* *be white as snow; though they are red like crimson, they shall* *be as wool."* Jesus wants us to run to Him rather than away from Him when we sin or miss the mark. We don't have to hide from Him the way Adam and Eve hid after they sinned in the Garden of Eden. We can actually come right to Him and talk with Him about our mistakes. It's a two-way discussion. We should not just make our confession, ask for forgiveness, and leave. We not only need His loving forgiveness and the cleansing that His precious blood has already secured for us; we need His advice and wisdom. We need His power. We need His grace! We need His divine influence in our hearts so that it can be reflected in our lives. We need grace to reign in our lives through Jesus, our Lord and Savior! Death came to humanity through Adam, but grace has come to us through Jesus Christ, as confirmed by Romans 5:17: *For by the one man's* *offense death reigned through the one, much more those who* *receive abundance of grace and of the gift of righteousness* *will reign in life through the One, Jesus Christ.*

The gospel truth is that grace, that divine influence in our hearts and its reflection in our lives, is much more powerful than sin. The key is to yield to it and let it reign in our lives. Listen to Paul's words in Romans 5:20-21: *Moreover the law* *entered that the offense might abound. But where sin abound-* *ed, grace abounded much more, so that as sin reigned in death,* *even so grace might reign through righteousness to eternal life* *through Jesus Christ our Lord.* As believers in Jesus, we are in right standing with God and we have access to the throne of His grace at all times. God has made provision through the throne of grace for the free gift of righteousness to be active in our lives. When we allow grace to reign in our lives, our righteousness is not hidden but is there for all to see.

I mentioned earlier that I had tried to free myself from alcoholism and substance abuse through the exercise of will power, but my fleshly efforts always eventually failed. I needed something more powerful than I could supply on my own. I needed God's grace. It was only when I humbled myself and asked for God's help that I received freedom. Upon my surrender to Jesus, I could actually feel the addictions leave me as the Spirit of Christ moved in. I knew I was free. I am still free. Not once have I gone back to the addictions. John put it this way in his gospel: *"Therefore if the Son makes you free, you shall be free indeed"* (John 8:36). "Free indeed" means genuinely free or truly free. However, we need to understand that freedom is a continual process.

Over these past thirty-six years since my new birth in Christ, I have spent much time sitting with Jesus in the gazebo of my heart that the Bible calls the "throne of grace." Physically, I may be sitting in an easy chair in the living room of my home, kneeling beside my bed, lying in my bed, or sitting at my desk; but spiritually I am in the gazebo of my heart. Most of the time when I meet with Him there, I have a Bible in my lap. Prayer and the Word of God go hand in hand.

Jesus said, *"If you abide in My word, you are my disciples indeed. And you shall know the truth, and the truth shall make you free"* (John 8:31b-32). Jesus, the gardener of our lives, uses His written word to make us free and keep us free. Digesting His word daily is a key way for God's grace to operate and grow in our lives. In John 6:63b, Jesus said, *"The words that I speak to you are spirit and they are life."* The words in the Bible are different than the words of any other book. The Scriptures are alive! They are spirit and they are life! His loving and powerful presence grows in us as we receive the seed of His word in our hearts and souls. With His presence comes freedom and liberty: *"Now the Lord is the Spirit; and where the Spirit of the Lord is, there is liberty"* (2 Corinthians 3:17).

Since I was set free from substance abuse, I have tried to help others fighting the same affliction. Over the years I have seen many delivered from their addictions. Some have stayed free, but some have tried to live on a roller coaster. One month they may be free and the next month back in bondage. When this happens, I have learned to ask the following question: "When did you stop reading your Bible and spending quality time with God?" Typically, there is a look of surprise on the face of the person being ministered to, as they wonder how I knew that they had abandoned their daily time with the Lord in His Word. Most often the answer to my question has been that the person stopped reading the Bible and spending quality time with God prior to returning to alcoholism or substance abuse. A big step on the road back to freedom is a recommitment to fellowship with Jesus in His Word and prayer. The person has to decide to assign top priority to spending time with Jesus, the great gardener of his or her life.

Thank God the tree of life for us is the cross of Christ. It's always available to us. It's there in our gardens by the throne of His grace. Repentance, the turning back to God, is not hidden. It's as easy as a trip to the gazebo. True repentance and confession is not merely standing off in the distance looking at the cross; it is coming back to the cross. It's a meeting and discussion with Jesus in the throne room of His grace.

Too often believers try to fight off the temptations and other attacks from our adversary, the devil, by relying solely on will power and their own strength rather than drawing on God's power. We need the power of the Holy Spirit, and we need the fruit of the Spirit to develop and grow in our lives. As we read in the previous chapter of this book, the fruit of the Spirit includes *"self-control"* (Galatians 5:22-23). The self-control described here is empowered by the Holy Spirit rather than by human will power. As we submit to and feed ourselves with the Word of God, our faith grows. Also the fruit of the Spirit, including self-control, grows in the gardens of our lives. Paul stated in Romans 10:17, *"So then faith comes by hearing, and hearing by the word of God."*

Romans 5:1-2 confirms that it is by faith that we access the grace we need for victory over the temptations of the evil one: *Therefore, having been justified by faith, we have peace with God through our Lord Jesus Christ, through whom also we have access by faith into this grace in which we stand, and rejoice in the hope of the glory of God.*

Spending time with God in His Word and in prayer plants more of the seeds of His Word in our spiritual gardens and also waters them. This beautiful process is described in Isaiah 55:10-13: *For as the rain comes down, and the snow from heaven, and do not return there, but water the earth, and make it bring forth and bud, that it may give seed to the sower and bread to the eater, so shall My word be that goes forth from My mouth; it shall not return to Me void, but it shall prosper in the thing for which I sent it. For you shall go out with joy, and be led out with peace; the mountains and the hills shall break forth into singing before you, and all the trees of the field shall clap their hands. Instead of the thorn shall come up the cypress tree, and instead of the brier shall come up the myrtle tree; and it shall be to the LORD for a name, for an everlasting sign that shall not be cut off.*

The Mediterranean cypress is a very tall tree that can live for over one thousand years. Myrtle trees contain essential oils that are healthy for the human body. It is easy to see the symbolism here. The sowing of God's Word into our lives brings spiritual, emotional, and physical health to us. It causes the witness of Christ to grow tall in our lives and to be noticed by others. It brings longevity of life. It waters the plants of God and chokes out the thorns and briers sown by our adversary.

The throne of His grace is a place of prayer where the power of God's love nourishes the very roots of His plants in the gardens of our lives. From Paul's prayer in Ephesians 3:14-21, we can see how God's power far exceeds anything our minds can produce on their own: *For this reason I bow my knees to the Father of our Lord Jesus Christ, from whom the whole family in heaven and earth is named, that He would grant you, according to the riches of His glory, to be strengthened with might through His Spirit in the inner man, that Christ may dwell in your hearts through faith; that you, being rooted and grounded in love, may be able to comprehend with all the saints what is the width and length and depth and height—to know the love of Christ which passes knowledge; that you may be filled with all the fullness of God. Now to Him who is able to do exceedingly abundantly above all we ask or think, according to the power that works in us, to Him be glory in the church by Christ Jesus to all generations, forever and ever. Amen.*

Being "rooted and grounded in love" makes for a healthy garden of life. We have to trust that God loves us, not on the basis of our works or the keeping of the law, but rather on the basis of Christ's works on the cross at Calvary. Paul put it this way in Galatians 5:6: *For in Christ Jesus neither circumcision nor uncircumcision avails anything, but faith working through love.* We have to trust in God's love in order to have a healthy spiritual garden. After all, the Father's motivation for sending His Son Jesus to the cross was His love for us: *For God so loved the world that He gave His only begotten Son, that whoever believes in Him should not perish but have everlasting life* (John 3:16). I do believe that the main reason God created us humans was to have fellowship with us. He is not mad at us! He loves us! He proved His love for us at a place called Calvary. Below are song lyrics that I wrote in 2005 as my way of expressing the proof of His love for us:

In My Heart to Stay

Verse 1

You proved Your love for me
At a place called Calvary
And You are in my heart to stay
You've touched my lonely soul
And filled my empty life
I put my trust in You always

Verse 2

You paid the price for me
When You died upon the tree
And You are in my heart to stay
You rescued me from sin
And took my punishment
I put my trust in You always

Verse 3

You conquered death for me
When You rose triumphantly
And You are in my heart to stay
You blew Your wind on me
And set my spirit free
I put my trust in You always

Chorus

And You are in my heart to say
And You are in my heart to stay
Yes, You are in my heart to stay[7]

"According to the riches of His glory" (another key phrase from Paul's prayer in Ephesians 3:14-21) is also very important in understanding the power of God's grace. The glory of God implies a manifestation of His powerful and majestic presence. When we come to Him with an attitude of humility, acknowledging our weaknesses and asking for His help, He is always there. He will not turn us away. David wrote in Psalm 51:17: *"The sacrifices of God are a broken spirit, a broken and a contrite heart – these, O God, You will not despise."*

King David was a man who knew how to meet with God. He even set up the ark of the covenant with its mercy seat in a tent or tabernacle near his palace. Only the high priest was supposed to be allowed in the presence of the ark, but God made an exception in the case of King David. David is in the lineage of Jesus Christ. Jesus is also referred to as the Son of David. David was clearly a type and foreshadow of the coming Messiah, Jesus, Who is our king, prophet, and high priest. We don't know how much time David spent in the tent with the ark of the covenant, but I believe he spent a lot of time there, as evidenced by the following verses from Psalms written by him:

For in the time of trouble He shall hide me in His pavilion; in the secret place of His tabernacle He shall hide me; He shall set me high upon a rock. And now my head shall be lifted up above my enemies all around me; therefore I will offer the sacrifices of joy in His tabernacle; I will sing, yes, I will sing praises to the LORD. Hear, O LORD, when I cry with my voice! Have mercy also upon me, and answer me. When You said, "Seek My face," my heart said to You, "Your face, LORD, I will seek." Do not hide Your face from me; do not turn Your face from me; do not turn Your servant away in anger; You have been my help; do not leave me nor forsake me, O God of my salvation (Psalm 27:5-9).

I will abide in Your tabernacle forever; I will trust in the shelter of Your wings. Selah (Psalm 61:4).

As indicated by the above verses, David rejoiced and sang praises to the Lord while in the tent with the ark of the covenant and its mercy seat. He very likely wrote some of his psalms while there surrounded with the presence and glory of God. Certainly, while in that tent, David experienced "the riches of His glory." I believe that David's tent was a prefigure of the throne of God's grace that is available to all New Testament believers today in the gardens of their hearts.

James, the brother of our Lord, really confirms this in his statement to the Jerusalem Council, as recorded in Acts 15:13-17: *And after they had become silent, James answered, saying, "Men and brethren, listen to me: Simon has declared how God at the first visited the Gentiles to take out of them a people for His name. And with this the words of the prophets agree, just as it is written: 'After this I will return and will rebuild the tabernacle of David, which has fallen down; I will rebuild its ruins, and will set it up; so that the rest of mankind may seek the LORD, even all the Gentiles who are called by My name, says the LORD who does all these things.'* "

The Jerusalem Council had met to discuss the question as to whether the Gentile believers were required to keep the Old Testament law and its rituals as a condition of their salvation. In the above verses James was saying that the Gentiles coming to God through Jesus Christ was a fulfillment of the rebuilding of the tabernacle of David which was a tent with a single compartment containing the ark of the covenant and the mercy seat. The tabernacle of Moses, and later the temple, each contained an outer court, a holy place, and a most holy place in which rested the ark and the mercy seat. Jesus was in Jerusalem (probably in the vicinity of the temple) when He said, *"I am the way, the truth, and the life. No one comes to the Father, except through Me"* (from John 14:6). The Jews actually referred to the outer court of the temple as "the Way." They referred to the holy place (the compartment containing the showbread, the candlestick, and the altar of incense) as the "the Truth." And they referred to the most holy place (the compartment which contained the ark of the covenant and the mercy seat) as "the Life." Jesus was clearly comparing the simplicity of His gospel to the rebuilding of the tabernacle of David. The only door we need to go through in order to access His throne of grace is Jesus Himself! Jesus said, *"I am the door. If anyone enters by Me, he will be saved, and will go in and out and find pasture"* (John 10:9).

Jesus is not only the door; He is the mercy seat itself. This is confirmed in 1 John 2:2: *And He Himself is the propitiation for our sins, and not for ours only but also for the whole world.* In the Septuagint, the Old Testament in Greek, the same word used here for "propitiation" is used for the mercy seat. It was on the mercy seat that the high priest sprinkled the blood of the Israelites' sacrifices (Exodus 25:17). John also confirms that Jesus is our mercy seat in 1 John 4:10: *In this is love, not that we loved God, but that He loved us and sent His Son to be the propitiation* [mercy seat] *for our sins.*

In summary, the throne of grace is available to all believers today. It is like a beautiful gazebo in the center of the gardens of our hearts. As the scripture says, we can go there boldly to obtain mercy and find grace to help in time of need (from Hebrews 4:16). The Lord wants to hear from us. He created us in order to have fellowship with us. He loves us and wants to spend time with us.

Too often believers are deceived into thinking that they would be better off not bothering God. They have been deceived into thinking that their going to the Lord with their sins, mistakes, weaknesses, problems and the like are troublesome to God. They think they are not important enough to take up God's valuable time. The truth is that God is not limited by time. He created the dimension of time and is not constrained by it. God is omnipresent in that He is everywhere at the same time. He is omniscient in that He knows everything. He is omnipotent in that He is all powerful. His power can not be used up or depleted. Your life is just as important to God as the life of the most famous person you can think of. Your life is just as important to God as the life of a king or president of a country. God is involved in your life and working providentially in it just as much as He is working in the life of the most listened to preacher on earth today. If you were to dip a large bucket in the ocean and fill it with water, would there be a measurable decrease in the ocean level? I think not. In like manner, our time in the throne room of His grace does not and cannot deplete Him. He is always there looking forward to our fellowship.

I offer the following prayer to help you to set a goal of making regular and frequent visits to that beautiful gazebo, the throne of grace, that the Lord has placed in the garden of your heart:

Dear Lord, I want to be like David who sought Your face with his whole heart. Just as the mercy seat was available to him in his tabernacle, I know that You are always there for me in the throne room of Your grace. Thank You for Your patient love and mercy. You may have noticed some weeds and briers growing in my garden. I look forward to Your pulling them out by their roots. Thank You for the grace You have extended to me. Forgive me for allowing the enemy to sow his seeds in my soil. I ask You for a crop failure on all of his seeds. I'm bringing my Bible with me when I visit with You. I ask You to plant the seeds of

Your Word in the garden of my heart. I look forward to the riches of Your glory being manifested in my life. I need Your face to shine upon me and provide nourishing light for my garden. I need Your presence, Your wisdom, Your power, and Your direction for my life. Most of all I need You. In the name of Jesus, I pray. Amen.

Chapter 4

The Power of Seeds

All of us have observed the power of natural seeds during our lifetimes. I remember as a young boy being amazed at how plants could breakthrough concrete in sidewalks and parking lots. Now, most contractors include the cost of an herbicide in their bids for concrete or asphalt paving. They are acknowledging the power of seeds.

As I mentioned earlier, every seed contains an embryo of the plant it will become. A pine seed lying beneath concrete is a pine tree waiting to breakthrough any minute crack it can find. Jesus said, *"If you have faith as a mustard seed, you will say to this mountain, 'Move from here to there,' and it will move; and nothing will be impossible for you"* (from Matthew 17:20). Natural seeds can break through concrete, but seeds of faith can split and level mountains!

Many years ago a well-known evangelist, whose ministry my wife Schar and I were supporting financially, sent us a newsletter that contained a very interesting proposal. Enclosed with the letter was a small packet of mustard seeds. Whether they were seeds for mustard plants or seeds for mustard trees like the ones that grow in Israel was not specified. The seeds were very small, like little black dots. The letter provided a return envelope and proposed that we send one seed back to the evangelist for each of our prayer requests. Each seed represented mustard seed faith and was a tangible way for the evangelist to put his faith and agreement with ours upon receipt of our prayer requests. While the evangelist's proposal was good and noble, we decided to do something else. We actually planted the seeds about one inch deep in a flowerpot full of rich, black soil. We wanted to see what these seeds would produce.

At that time, we had a pet dog named Rachel. She was a beautiful Lhasa Apso. We had placed the flowerpot containing the black soil and mustard seeds on the back porch where it could get plenty of sunlight. It didn't take long for Rachel to knock the flowerpot over and scatter its contents. It looked as though our experiment was doomed. There was no way to distinguish between the black soil and the small black seeds, so we could not replant the seeds at a uniform depth. We just scooped the whole mess up, put it back in the pot and forgot about it. Some days later we were amazed to find the whole surface of the flowerpot covered with little green plants!

God taught Schar and me a lesson from that experience. Even though we do our best to plant the seeds of God's Word in the gardens of our lives, sometimes unforeseen things occur that overturn all our plans and scatter our faith. When that happens, we need to remember that the seeds of the Word of God are under the control of Jesus Christ Who is the Word. He is also the master farmer of our lives. When things look like a mess, His grace is still there working to bring in a good crop from the soil of our hearts, if we do not give up. As long as we don't quit, the Lord has something with which to work.

It also helps to remind ourselves that God's grace acts on the merits of Jesus Christ rather than on our own merits and is activated by faith (Romans 5:2). Even when we've made a mess of things, we have not made a mess of the grace of God. It is still there working beneath the soil, repositioning the seeds of God's Word for breakthrough, if we will only believe. The Lord of the breakthrough is also the Lord of grace!

When Zerubbabel was governor of Israel during its first regathering, he was responsible for seeing that the temple in Jerusalem was rebuilt. The work was slow, and there was much discouragement. There was also much opposition from the neighboring Samaritans who had been able to persuade the Persian government to give an order to halt construction. Apathy and lethargy had set in among God's people, but around 520 B.C., God used the prophet Zechariah to bring encouragement and divine energy back into the project. Zechariah 4:6-7 recounts part of a message given to Zechariah by an angel for Zerubbabel, the governor: *So he answered and said to me: "This is the word of the LORD to Zerubbabel: 'not by might nor by power, but by My Spirit,' says the LORD of hosts. 'Who are you, O great mountain? Before Zerubbabel you shall become a plain! And he shall bring forth the capstone with shouts of "Grace, grace to it!"'*

God was sending a message to the governor, Zerubbabel, and to all the regathered Jews, that it's not by any man's might, and it's not by any man's power, that mountains of opposition are leveled; it is by the power of the Holy Spirit! If we will only believe, grace will reign, and grace will prevail! And God will get all the glory! When the final stone, the capstone, is put in place in any Spirit-led project of our lives, we too can shout, "Grace, grace to it!" By this, I believe we are acknowledging that it was built by grace and that it will continue with God's grace, with His favor, and with His blessing! When facing opposition and discouragement, we should always remember that faith the size of a mustard seed can access grace that is bigger than any mountain! Instead of bowing down to the mountain, we need to bow down to God, knowing that one seed from His Word can level any mountain of opposition to His plans for our lives. Once He gives us the Word, we need to plant it by speaking it to the mountain. In this way, we are activating the grace of God by faith. Again, Jesus said, *"If you have faith as a mustard seed, you will say to this mountain, 'Move from here to there,' and it will move; and nothing will be impossible for you"* (from Matthew 17:20). I've heard it said that too often believers talk to God about how big the mountain is when, really, they should talk to the mountain about how big God is!

One of the biggest mountains that Christians face during their lifetimes is the mountain of unforgiveness. It can block the flow of grace in a believer's life if he or she does not deal with it. It's interesting that the inner man is often referred to as the heart in the Bible. Since one's physical heart is a pump, it is reasonable to assume that the inner man is similar to a pump. Just as the physical heart receives blood in and pumps blood out, the spiritual heart of man receives God's grace in and pumps it out. If there is a blockage in the flow of blood through a person's heart, a heart attack occurs. In like manner, if there is a blockage in the flow of God's grace through one's spiritual heart, a spiritual heart attack occurs. Too many Christians today are in a state of spiritual cardiac arrest.

Just as physical heart attacks are painful and immobilizing, spiritual heart attacks hurt and restrict the inner man. One cause of a physical heart attack is the buildup of plaque in the arteries. Unforgiveness, if it is not dealt with, acts like a spiritual plaque that builds up and hinders the flow of grace in the believer's inner man. Unforgiveness in the Christian's spiritual heart will eventually place him or her in a state of spiritual cardiac arrest, which is painful and immobilizing to the inner man and can even result in the death of a marriage, a ministry, a career, a friendship, or some other area of that person's life. But, thank God, Jesus has given us in His Word a way to remove spiritual plaque! Listen to His words in Mark 11:22-26:

So Jesus answered and said to them, "Have faith in God. For assuredly, I say to you, whoever says to this mountain, 'Be removed and be cast into the sea,' and does not doubt in his heart, but believes that those things he says will be done, he will have whatever he says. Therefore I say to you, whatever things you ask when you pray, believe that you receive them, and you will have them. And whenever you stand praying, if you have anything against anyone, forgive him, that your Father in heaven may also forgive you your trespasses. But if you do not forgive, neither will your Father in heaven forgive your trespasses."

Notice that Jesus uses the word "say" or "says" a total of five times in the above verses. He is giving us a powerful clue as to how we can remove the plaque of unforgiveness from the arteries of our inner persons. We begin by acknowledging that the unforgiveness is a real obstacle. It is a mountain that keeps us in a prison of hurt and blocks God's plans for our lives. Next, we cast the mountain into the sea by saying aloud that we forgive the person who hurt us. Most of the time we don't feel like forgiving the person, but notice that Jesus does not base His advice to us on how we feel. His advice is based on the words that we speak. Forgiveness is not a feeling; it is a decision. The fact that we don't feel like forgiving the person is the very reason that we need to forgive him or her. Jesus is assuring us here that He will meet us right where we are. If we will speak to the mountain and say that we forgive the person, Jesus will cause the words of our mouths to become truth in our hearts.

When I forgive, I say aloud that I forgive the person, and then I ask the Lord to cause the words of my mouth to become truth in my heart. Many times, I have forgiven and gone to sleep with wrong feelings still in my heart, only to awake with the animosity gone. God removed the spiritual plaque from my inner man while I slept. What a blessing!

Words are powerful seeds. Proverbs 18:21 tells us, *"Death and life are in the power of the tongue, and those who love it will eat its fruit."*

All my life I have heard people say, "Sticks and stones may break my bones, but words will never hurt me." This saying is so very wrong! Words can hurt. They can even bring death. But, if used correctly, words can bring life!

Moses quoted God as saying, *"I have set before you life and death, blessing and cursing; therefore choose life"* (from Deuteronomy 30:19). When it comes to unforgiveness, we have a choice to make. We can follow the advice of Jesus and speak to the mountain of unforgiveness or we can let it continue to grow, thereby blocking God's plans for our lives. Choose life! Speak to the mountain in the name of Jesus and cast it into the sea. There are actually mountains underneath the ocean, but they do not have names, or if they do, we never hear of them. Mountains of unforgiveness are cast into a sea of forgetfulness.

Other mountains we need to speak to might be mountains of oppression, discouragement, addiction, sickness, poverty, fear, and the like. The number one preacher we hear over our lifetimes is not our pastor, nor our favorite television minister, evangelist, or teacher. The number one preacher one hears is oneself. We cannot escape our own words. Every word we speak is a seed. When facing sickness, we can sow a seed of healing by quoting a verse from the Bible on healing and proclaiming it over ourselves. For example, Psalm 103:1-3 states: *Bless the LORD, O my soul; and all that is within me, bless His holy name! Bless the LORD, O my soul, and forget not all His benefits: Who forgives all your iniquities, Who heals all your diseases.* This verse covers "all diseases." It's always good to bring the merits of Jesus into our preaching to ourselves. In facing a mountain of sickness, a person might say, "By the stripes of Jesus I was healed (Isaiah 53:5 and 1 Peter 2:24). Jesus took those stripes on His back and carried them to the cross for my healing. The price has already been paid by the works of Jesus at Calvary. Healing is beginning now in my body!" If a person will continue to sow the seed of God's Word concerning his need, eventually he will believe it, and grace will be activated. *"So then faith comes by hearing, and hearing by the word of God"* (Romans 10:17). The key is to find the place where it is written regarding one's need and then to plant the seed by speaking the Word. God's written Word contains seeds for every basic area of human need. Following are some more examples:

Salvation: John 3:16: *For God so loved the world that He gave His only begotten Son, that whoever believes in Him should not perish but have everlasting life.* Romans 10:9-10, 13: *That if you confess with your mouth the Lord Jesus and believe in your heart that God has raised Him from the dead, you will be saved. For with the heart one believes unto righteousness, and with the mouth confession is made unto salvation. For "whoever calls on the name of the LORD shall be saved."*

Deliverance from fear: 1 John 4:18a: *There is no fear in love; but perfect love casts out fear, because fear involves torment.* 2 Timothy 1:7: *For God has not given us a spirit of fear, but of power and of love and of a sound mind.*

Peace: Philippians 4:6-7: *Be anxious for nothing, but in everything by prayer and supplication, with thanksgiving, let your requests be made known to God; and the peace of God, which surpasses all understanding, will guard your hearts and minds through Christ Jesus.* Isaiah 26:3: *You will keep him in perfect peace, whose mind is stayed on You, because he trusts in You.*

Joy: Romans 14:17: *For the kingdom of God is not eating and drinking but righteousness and peace and joy in the Holy Spirit.* Nehemiah 8:10b: *Do not sorrow, for the joy of the LORD is your strength.* Psalm 118:24: *This is the day the LORD has made; we will rejoice and be glad in it.* Psalm 30:5b: *Weeping may endure for a night, but joy comes in the morning.* Philippians 4:4: *Rejoice in the Lord always. Again I will say, rejoice!*

Many of the parables told by Jesus in the New Testament are agricultural in nature and steer us toward viewing our hearts and lives as gardens for the planting of the seeds of His Word. Grace, the divine influence in our hearts and its reflection in our lives, is activated by faith which grows as we receive the sowing of the seeds of His Word into the soils of our hearts. The rate at which God's paradise grows within us and prevails in our lives is determined largely by the type of soil we make available to Him. The parable of the soils told by Jesus in Matthew 13:3-9 helps us to understand this principle:

Then He spoke many things to them in parables, saying: "Behold, a sower went out to sow. And as he sowed, some seed fell by the wayside; and the birds came and devoured them. Some fell on stony places, where they did not have much earth; and immediately sprang up because they had no depth of earth. But when the sun was up they were scorched, and because they had no root they withered away. And some fell among thorns, and the thorns sprang up and choked them. But others fell on good ground and yielded a crop: some a hundredfold, some sixty, some thirty. He who has ears to hear, let him hear!"

In Matthew 13:18-23, Jesus explains the meaning of this parable: *Therefore hear the parable of the sower: When anyone hears the word of the kingdom, and does not understand it, then the wicked one comes and snatches away what was sown in his heart. This is he who received seed by the wayside. But*

*he who received the seed on stony places, this is he who hears
the word and immediately receives it with joy; yet he has no
root in himself, but endures only for a while. For when tribulation or persecution arises because of the word, immediately
he stumbles. Now he who received seed among thorns is he
who hears the word, and the cares of this world and the deceitfulness of riches choke the word, and he becomes unfruitful.
But he who received seed on good ground is he who hears the
word and understands it, who indeed bears fruit and produces: some a hundredfold, some sixty, some thirty.*

Not hearing the Word of God correctly and not understanding it makes for unproductive soil in the garden of one's life.
At the beginning of this book I wrote that, as a young boy, I
was not able to bring watermelons to maturity in the heavy
red soil of our backyard. I found out later that watermelons
need light sandy soil to grow well. In the same way, we cannot
bring the fruit of God's Word to maturity in our lives without the right kind of soil. Jesus, in the above verses, identified
three areas of misunderstanding that can contaminate the soil
of one's heart.

The first type of unproductive ground is soil by the wayside. This soil has been subjected to a lot of traffic which has
hardened it and made it difficult for the seeds of God's Word to
penetrate it. The seeds lie on the surface and are easily picked
up and devoured by various birds. These birds represent the
devil and lying, demonic spirits. The traffic that has hardened
the soil of this person's heart could be man-made philoso-
phies, false religions (including universalism, the New Age
movement, and a growing false theology of so-called aliens),
false sciences such as evolution, the many deceptions of sec-
ular humanism, political correctness, intellectualism, relative
ethics and morality, witchcraft, astrology, and the occult. This
type of soil does not understand and value the sacredness of

God's Word. This person needs to post a "no trespassing" sign to thoughts and ideas that disagree with the absolute truth of the Word of God.

I can personally say that, at the same time I accepted Jesus Christ as my personal Lord and Savior, I also accepted the Bible as the absolute truth. I thank God that the Holy Spirit prompted me to include this decision with my surrender. It has kept my heart soft and ready to receive the seeds of God's Word every day.

The second type of unproductive soil is referred to in the parable as "stony places." This is a shallow layer of topsoil over a bed of rock. The seeds germinated and sprang up quickly as the rock kept moisture near the surface and radiated the warmth of the sun back up through the soil. But the plants could only live for a short time because the roots of the plants could not penetrate the layer of stone. Healthy plants have deep roots that reach down into the cool depths of the earth, drawing in moisture and keeping the plant from burning and drying up when there is no rainfall, the morning dew is gone, and the sun is at its height. This soil typifies the person who likes the message of grace (unmerited favor and blessing) but has kept a stone door locked over the vault of his heart. He likes the message but has refused to accept the messenger.

In Revelation 3:20, Jesus said, "*Behold, I stand at the door and knock. If anyone hears my voice and opens the door, I will come in to him and dine with him, and he with Me.*" The person typified by "stony places" gladly listens to the Word of God but does not open the door of his heart to Jesus, the author and finisher of his faith. He knows about Jesus, but he does not know Jesus. He does not have a personal relationship with the Lord. When persecution or tribulation occurs because of the Word (that is because he looks favorably upon the Word and likes it) he stumbles when challenged about the Word. He does not know the author, Jesus, and does not have the deep-rooted strength to stand with Him when the heat of persecution and tribulation arises.

Most of the time we do not know the authors of books we read. By that, I mean that we do not have personal relationships with them. I may like a book, but if I do not know the author, I might have difficulty defending its authenticity if challenged. Well, the author of the Word of God wants us all to have a personal relationship with Him. He knocks on the door of every heart, wanting to come in and dine. He wants to take up residence in us. He wants all of us to know Him personally. Jeremiah, in prophesying about the New Covenant, said, *"No more shall every man teach his neighbor, saying, 'Know the LORD,' for they shall all know Me, from the least of them to the greatest of them, says the LORD"* (from Jeremiah 31:34). The "stony places" represents the man or woman who might know the letter of the Word but does not really know the Person of the Word.

I remember some of the reactions of people after I surrendered my heart to Jesus on Sunday, February 24, 1985. Everyone at work knew I was a Christian within a few minutes after I walked into my office the next morning. By the end of my first week as a believer, most of my family, friends, and acquaintances knew I was a Christian. From the time I came to Christ, I have always been very vocal about my faith. I quickly learned that while some folks were very happy about my conversion, there were others who hated me for it. Some practiced the old back-stabbing tactics that I believe come straight from the devil. Here in the United States, this behind the back persecution is the most common, although frontal assaults from the enemy are becoming more frequent as our nation has degenerated more and more into secularism. Then there were others who were just curious. I tried to witness to them all, and by the grace of God I have continued to tell others about Jesus.

Interestingly, through the years, I have seen some of those who persecuted me eventually come to the cross with their lives. No one is over a decision away from having a personal relationship with God. The Apostle Paul was one of the worst enemies of the church before his conversion on the road to Damascus. Oh, how wonderful is the saving power of our Lord Jesus Christ!

I got saved during the oil bust of the 1980s and being the CEO of an oil company, I faced some severe tests. At the same time, I knew that God had called me into fulltime ministry. In my first weeks as a believer, I remember fighting discouragement because of some of the persecutions and tribulations I was experiencing. While driving my car home from work one day, I was hurting from some unpleasant encounters with antagonistic people when I felt a hand of assurance on the back of my shoulder. I knew in my heart that it was the hand of Jesus. I was so sure that it was His hand that I was afraid to look in the rearview mirror. His touch healed the bruises of my persecutions and tribulations, and that was enough. We cannot stand against our spiritual enemy, the accuser of the brethren, without a personal relationship with the all-powerful Lord and Savior of mankind, Jesus Christ. Without Him, we are simply stony ground.

The third type of unproductive ground that Jesus discussed in His parable is soil covered with thorns. As Jesus explained, this represents persons who bring no fruit to maturity from the seed of the Word of God because of the cares of this world and the deceitfulness of riches. This person values material things over spiritual things. Things seem to go okay for them until they have to choose between a spiritual value and a material value. There's an old saying: "God doesn't mind us having money; He just doesn't want our money to have us." When a person lets money reign in his heart, he will ultimately make many decisions that are contrary to the moral directives of the Word of God. Jesus said, *"No one can serve two masters; for either he will hate the one and love the other, or else he will be loyal to the one and despise the other. You cannot serve God and mammon"* (Matthew 6:24). If we let mammon sit on the throne of our hearts, we will ultimately see a garden of thorns rather than the fruit of the Spirit.

One of the most misquoted verses in the Bible is 1 Timothy 6:10: *For the love of money is a root of all kinds of evil, for which some have strayed from the faith in their greediness, and have pierced themselves through with many sorrows.* The world (especially in Hollywood movie scripts) likes to say, "Money is the root of all evil." However, there is a huge error in saying simply "money" rather than the "love of money." The underlying motive of this massive misquote is to encourage all Christians to be poor. The devil knows we need money to do things like care for our families, support the local church, support missionaries and other ministries, print Bibles, publish Christian literature, care for widows and orphans, help the poor, and all the other loving and charitable deeds that God has called His people to do. As sound believers, we need to be careful not to fall in love with our money and material possessions. We do not love money; we use money to help those we love. Our money does not manage us; we manage our money. We do not trust in riches; we trust in God, recognizing Him as our provider.

The good soil described by Jesus in His parable is the person who hears the Word of God, understands it, and bears fruit up to a hundredfold. Unlike the hardened soil by the wayside, this person receives the seeds from God's Word as being the absolute truth and has posted a "no trespassing" sign to information that disagrees with the Scriptures. This person has the highest regard for the sacredness of the Holy Bible. Unlike the stony ground, the person represented by good soil has made a complete surrender to Jesus, has experienced His love on a continuing basis, and understands that God's Word is a love letter to him or her. This person's heart is deeply rooted in the love of God. This person places spiritual value over material things, and if he or she feels the slightest prick from the deceitfulness of riches or the cares of this world, a fire goes out from the throne of grace in the garden of his or her heart. Thorns burn quickly and easily!

In the next chapter, "The Mathematics of Grace," we will examine, among other things, the hundredfold return. But first, I offer the following prayer to help you make an important commitment to sow daily the powerful seeds of God's Word into the soil of the garden of your life:

Heavenly Father, I believe that the Bible is a seed packet gifted to me as part of my inheritance in Christ. I commit myself to the sowing of the powerful seeds of your Word daily into the soil of my heart. I ask for your help in keeping the soil of my heart tilled and ready to receive, knowing that even when I fail, Your grace has not failed, and the seeds of Your Word will produce a harvest in my life. I pray this in the name of Your Son Jesus. Amen.

Chapter 5

The Mathematics of Grace

In the last chapter, we read from the parable of the soils (Matthew 13) that the good ground produced up to a "hundredfold" return. Examining the "hundredfold" return leads us into the exciting realm of the mathematics of grace.

Typically, "hundredfold" is defined as one hundred times, and this could be the intended meaning. Yet, if this is true, why tack on the word "fold?" It could be that Jesus meant a number that results from literally folding something 100 times. If I take a piece of paper and fold it once, I have 2 squares formed by the creases in the paper; if I fold it twice, I have 4 squares; if I fold it three times I have 8 squares; if I fold it four times, I have 16 squares; if I fold it five times, I have 32 squares; if I fold it six times, I have 64 squares; if I fold it seven times, I have 128 squares; if I fold it 8 times, I have 256 squares, if I fold it 9 times, I have 512 squares, if I fold it 10 times, I have 1,024 squares, if I fold it 11 times, I have 2,048 squares; if I fold it 12 times, I have 4,096 squares; 20 times would be 1,048,576; 25 times would be 33,554,432; 30 times would be 1,053,741,824. If I were to be able to fold it 100 times, I would have to spend the rest of my life counting the squares. The number of squares would be so large, I could not write it down in the normal way. It would be greater than trillions and zillions. I would have to go to one of my old math books from college and review how to write the number exponentially. I suppose that the most exciting aspect of the hundredfold return is that it obviously must continue into one's afterlife in order to be completely fulfilled. It points to eternity and brings home the enormous potential of every believer's garden of grace.

The mathematics of grace is different in many respects from the mathematics of the world. For example, the world looks on increase as being a result of addition. But Jesus said in Luke 6:38: *"Give, and it will be given to you: good measure, pressed down, shaken together, and running over will be put into your bosom. For with the same measure that you use, it will be measured back to you."* In this verse we see that increase actually comes through subtraction rather than addition. We might even say that in the mathematics of grace, we add through subtraction. Growth comes through giving rather than getting.

Farmers understand grace's system of math better than most because they employ it every growing season. A farmer knows that he must prepare and till his land. He also knows that no matter how hard he works, there will be no crop unless he sows his seeds. He knows that he must give seeds to the land in order to reap a harvest. He understands adding through subtraction.

Grace, that gift of unmerited favor and divine influence in our hearts paid for by the precious blood of Jesus, is agricultural in nature. Grace came to humanity in a Seed. That Seed is Jesus Christ (Galatians 3:16). In John 12, Andrew and Philip told Jesus that some Greeks, who had come to Jerusalem to worship at the feast of Passover, wanted to see Him. Jesus knew that His Father planned on giving Him a harvest that would cover the entire world and extend to all people in every generation. He took the request of these Greeks as a sign that the time had come for His crucifixion. The time had come for the Seed to be planted. This is evident by His response: *But Jesus answered them, saying, "The hour has come that the Son of Man should be glorified. Most assuredly, I say to you, unless a grain of wheat falls into the ground and dies, it remains alone; but if it dies, it produces much grain"* (John 12:23-24). The grain of wheat that died at Calvary about 2,000 years ago is continuing to produce the grain of born-again believers all over the earth! The potential of every born-again believer to produce more grain becomes very exciting when we consider the mathematics of grace.

The following information on wheat statistics is gleaned from an online article published by The University of Arizona: One grain or kernel of wheat, when planted, germinates and produces a plant which is called a stalk. Each stalk has 3 to 12 stems which are called tillers. At the top of each tiller is a head which contains about 50 grains of wheat. There are about 15,000 to 17,000 grains in a pound. A bushel of wheat weighs about 60 pounds. A bushel yields about 60 pounds of whole wheat flour or about 42 pounds of white flour. One bushel of wheat, when additional ingredients are added, bakes into 90 one-pound loaves of whole-wheat bread or makes 72 pounds of flour tortillas or rolls into 420 three-ounce cinnamon rolls or makes 5,000 four-inch cookies.[8]

A grain of wheat does not appear to be very valuable when we look at it. When compared to a one carat diamond, which has a median value today of about $5,000, a grain of wheat would appear to be worthless. Most of us would choose the diamond over the grain of wheat any day. But let's think about it. One hundred years from now, the diamond will still be worth about $5,000 with adjustments for inflation. If we plant the grain of wheat and continually harvest and replant each season's crop, we will have much more value than $5,000 at the

end of 100 years. From the range of 3 to 12 stems or tillers
from a grain of wheat, we'll choose 7, which is approximately
in the middle of the range given in the University of Arizona
study. Interestingly, in Pharaoh's dream interpreted by Joseph
in Genesis 41, each wheat stalk contained 7 heads. So, at the
end of the first year, our one grain of wheat will produce a harvest of 7 heads of wheat of about 50 grains per head. This gives
us a harvest of 350 grains after the first year. Planting all 350
grains gives us a harvest of 350 times 350 for a total of 122,500
grains at the end of year two. Using 16,000 grains to a pound,
we have about 7.7 pounds of wheat at the end of year two.
Continuing to replant all of our wheat grain harvest, we have
about 2,695 pounds or about 44.9 bushels of wheat, enough to
make 224,500 four-inch cookies, at the end of year three. At
the end of year four, we have about 15,715 bushels, enough to
make 6,600,300 three-ounce cinnamon rolls, and at the end of
year five 5,500,250 bushels. In recent years, wheat prices have
averaged about $5 per bushel. Amazingly, at the end of only
five years, our original grain of wheat has grown to a yearly
harvest value of over 27 million dollars! Continuing our replanting and harvest, we would have a wheat harvest value of
$9,450,000,000 at the end of year 6 and $3,307,500,000,000
at the end of year 7. To write the harvest value after 100 years
would require exponential numbering. The $5,000 value of the
one carat diamond would be unchanged except for inflationary
adjustments. The diamond now pales in comparison to the value of the grain of wheat.

Of course, to accommodate such a massive agricultural
project would require the entire earth and many laborers. Yes,
Jesus knew that He was the Seed through which God's amazing grace was to come to the earth, and He also knew that the
resulting harvest would require many laborers in every generation. For example, listen to these instructions He gave to His

disciples in Matthew 9:37-38: *Then He said to His disciples, "The harvest truly is plentiful, but the laborers are few. Therefore pray the Lord of the harvest to send out laborers into His harvest."*

Matthew 28:18-20 describes this massive worldwide harvest and the Great Commission which all of us are called to participate in as laborers in the harvest fields of our generation: *And Jesus came and spoke to them, saying, "All authority has been given to Me in heaven and on earth. Go therefore and make disciples of all the nations, baptizing them in the name of the Father and of the Son and of the Holy Spirit, teaching them to observe all things that I have commanded you; and lo, I am with you always, even to the end of the age." Amen.*

As we study God's grace, it becomes apparent that it is not stagnant. Grace flows into a believer's heart with a divine mathematical plan to reproduce its Seed exponentially. It comes in with a shout of "sow!" As I shared earlier in this book, when I surrendered my heart to Jesus, I immediately began to tell others of His wonderful love and how He had rescued me from my sins, including the addictions that had imprisoned me. Personal testimonies are very effective ways to share the Gospel. Truly, every believer has the potential to be an "epistle of Christ" (2 Corinthians 3:3). I was a new believer and did not have all the answers to theological questions, but I had something real. I had a personal testimony. It has been said that a person with a real experience will always win out over someone who only has an argument.

In John chapter 9, Jesus healed and gave sight to a man who had been blind from birth. Because he was healed on a Sabbath, he was brought before a religious council of the Pharisees who interrogated him with many questions. I love the answer the formerly blind man gave in John 9:9: *He answered and said, "Whether He is a sinner or not I do not know. One thing I know that though I was blind, now I see."*

The formerly blind man had an experience that he knew was real. The Pharisees were faced with an undeniable truth that Jesus had given sight to a man who had been blind from birth. All of their blasphemies could not undo that real experience and its witness to many that day and its continued witness to us through the Scriptures. We are all learning from God's Word, but we don't always have the answer to every question. But like the blind man who was healed, we can all testify that though we once were blind, now we see! Every time we share our testimonies with others, we are sowing the Seed of Christ!

I encourage all who read this book to not delay in the sowing of your testimonies and to not use lack of preparation as an excuse. Paul pleaded with the Corinthians not to receive the grace of God in vain and to understand that now is the accepted time and that now is the day of salvation. *We then, as workers together with Him also plead with you not to receive the grace of God in vain. For He says: "In an acceptable time I have heard you, and in the day of salvation I have helped you." Behold, now is the accepted time; behold, now is the day of salvation* (2 Corinthians 6:1-2).

Sam Martin was a precious man of God. He is the person who led Pastor John Osteen to Jesus. He wrote a book entitled How I Led One and One Led a Million.[9] In his book he tells the story of how, as a teenager, he led his best friend John to the Lord. Pastor John Osteen over his lifetime was responsible for millions coming to Jesus for salvation. Not only was he the founder of the great Lakewood Church of Houston, Texas, which is one of the largest local churches in America, he also brought untold numbers to Christ in other nations. His son, Rev. Joel Osteen, pastors the church today and is continuing this great harvest of souls. It's obvious from his book and its title, Sam understood the mathematics of grace.

While I did not get saved through John Osteen's ministry, my family and I began attending Lakewood Church shortly after my conversion. We sat under his ministry for about ten years. During that time Pastor Osteen, more than anyone else, imparted a world vision to us. We did the work of evangelism while we were at Lakewood and led thousands to Jesus in the United States and in other countries. We held evangelistic meetings on the streets, in stadiums, in hotels, in fields, and wherever God opened the door. We also preached in churches, Full Gospel Business Men's Fellowship International (FGBMFI) meetings (including state, national, and world conferences), and Women's Aglow International meetings. We even got invited to be interviewed and to preach many times on various Christian television programs. FGBMFI's *Voice* magazine, which had a monthly circulation of about 600,000, selected my personal testimony for its cover story. It also appeared on its cover again for its 40-year anniversary issue. In 1995, we founded The Lord's Glory Church, which is a much smaller church than Lakewood. While our membership may not be in the thousands, we continue to reach out all over the world through the live streaming of our services, through our books, through our missions program, and through our members and their ministries. The Lord's Glory Church is just one of many ministries and churches that have been birthed at Lakewood Church. Sam Martin's harvest continues!

Early on, I learned to add the giving out of salvation tracts to my personal witness for Christ. A few years later I started writing Christian books. All of my books are full of Bible verses and include salvation prayers. I look on each book as a seed packet. About thirty years ago, I handed one of my books, <u>Face the Solution</u>, to a man in the parking lot of a shopping center here in Humble, Texas, and I never saw him again. I got a phone call about twenty years later from a lady who was a good friend of the man. She told me he had died and that he had left instructions with her to contact me. The address on the back of the book was no longer current, but she managed to find me. He had requested that I preach his funeral. She told me that he had prayed the prayer of salvation in the book I had given him. He had been living in his van which he kept parked in that same parking lot where I met him twenty years earlier. Immediately after his salvation experience, he began to hand out salvation tracts in that parking lot and continued to do so for twenty years. The shop owners in the shopping center liked him because he was like a free security guard. He would call the police if he saw anyone trying to break in or vandalize at night. Through my book, the man had received the Seed of Christ in his heart, and then for twenty years, he continued to sow the Seed of Christ by handing out salvation tracts.

The man was a veteran. As I preached his funeral service at Houston National Cemetery, I thought of how nice it would have been to have developed a friendship with him. The church I pastor is only about two miles from that parking lot, but he didn't know it because my family and I founded the church some years later. We used a post office box for an address on the back of the book. Not long after I gave him the book, that post office closed. But praise God, heaven's address doesn't change, and I will have all eternity to visit with my precious brother in Christ! Only in heaven will we realize the full impact of our witness. The mathematics of grace go far beyond our imaginations!

Not long after I was saved, I was invited to give my testimony and minister at the downtown Houston chapter of Full Gospel Business Men Fellowship International (FGBMFI). It was a luncheon meeting held at a centrally located hotel. I was very excited the night before the meeting. Instead of sleeping, I stayed awake, praying in the Spirit. The meeting was well attended with lots of downtown businesspeople, both men and women, dropping in on their lunch hour. People lined up for prayer after I spoke. I felt the presence of the Holy Spirit so strongly that it was as though I was standing in a cloud! My wife Schar stood with me as we prayed for each one. One lady wanted prayer for deliverance from cocaine addiction. We laid hands on her in the name of Jesus. We bowed our heads as we prayed and were astounded to see her empty shoes. Raising our heads, we saw her body laid out on the floor about six feet from us. The power of the Holy Spirit had knocked her right out of her shoes! Incredibly, her shoes had not moved an inch! She eventually got up from the floor proclaiming her deliverance and giving glory to God!

Many years later, after we had founded The Lord's Glory Church, a visitor told us that he had recently attended a service in a church located in the Third Ward of Houston. He said that the lady who had founded the church and was pastoring it with her husband shared during her sermon how she had been delivered from cocaine addiction at that downtown FGBMFI luncheon meeting years earlier. My wife and I had no idea of the far-reaching results of our prayer for that lady until the man reported it to us. We give Jesus all the glory and thank Him for the mathematics of grace operating in our ministry!

A visiting preacher at The Lord's Glory Church shared how his alcoholic parents had been saved. After an evening of drinking, they went into a diner for breakfast. Someone had left a salvation tract between the salt and pepper shakers. Still in a state of drunkenness, they read the tract, said the prayer, and were saved and delivered from alcoholism. After that experience they eventually became ordained ministers of the Gospel. Previous to that event, there had been no born-again believers in their family for several generations. The visiting preacher shared with us that he was one of over a hundred ordained ministers in his extended family. It all began with a salvation tract between a salt and pepper shaker. As I recall, they still don't know who left the tract there. But God knows, and we will all know when Jesus returns with His rewards in hand!

What may seem like a small act of obedience can result in an enormous, unimaginable return because of the wonderful mathematics of grace! Those small nudges of the Holy Spirit, if acted upon, can result in exponential returns! Seeds are small, but without them there is no harvest. Every time we plant the Seed of Jesus Christ, whether it be through a tract, the sharing of one's testimony, the sharing of the Scriptures, praying for someone in need, or just being a living letter of Christ, we may be planting a whole forest in God's kingdom because of the mathematics of His grace!

I offer the following prayer to help you to claim by faith the great potential of every seed you plant in God's harvest field:

Father God, I ask you to give me a world vision of harvest for your kingdom. May I see the great potential of every eternal seed I sow into the soil of humanity. I declare that I am walking by faith rather than by sight and that, even when I don't see the results, the mathematics of grace are operating. May the garden of paradise that you have placed in my heart become a center for sowing the good news of Jesus to lost and hurting people. In my heart may I always hear the voice of grace crying out "Sow!" I pray this in the name of Your Son Jesus. Amen.

Chapter 6

Grace in Giving

There is a great misconception among many Christians concerning money. They have been led to believe that talk of the giving of tithes and offerings is a brand of legalism rather than grace. Let's see what the Bible says. We'll start with 2 Corinthians 8:1-7:

1 Moreover, brethren, we make known to you the grace of God bestowed on the churches of Macedonia: 2 that in a great trial of affliction the abundance of their joy and their deep poverty abounded in the riches of their liberality. 3 For I bear witness that according to their ability, yes, and beyond their ability, they were freely willing, 4 imploring us with much urgency that we would receive the gift and the fellowship of the ministering to the saints. 5 And not only as we had hoped, but they first gave themselves to the Lord, and then to us by the will of God. 6 So we urged Titus, that as he had begun, so he would also complete this grace in you as well. 7 But as you abound in everything--in faith, in speech, in knowledge, in all diligence, and in your love for us--see that you abound in this grace also.

In the above text, Paul was encouraging the Corinthians to follow the example of the Macedonians in their giving of offerings to help the believers in Jerusalem. Even though the

Macedonians were experiencing persecution that had caused them much affliction and poverty, they actually pleaded with Paul to allow them to give into his ministry for the saints in Jerusalem. Their giving was certainly not motivated by legalism. Paul referred to their very act of giving as "this grace" (verses 6 and 7). Paul identifies the source of their grace as being God Himself in verse 1. This text beautifully illustrates the definition of grace given by Strong's and cited earlier in chapter 2 of this book as "the divine influence upon the heart, and its reflection in the life."[10] The Macedonians wanted to give because, as Paul put it in verse 5, they had given themselves to the Lord. It was the Spirit of Christ within them, influencing them. Their giving was the reflection of the presence of Jesus in their lives! Their act of giving was grace itself!

After all, God is the biggest giver of all. John 3:16 beautifully describes God's giving heart: *"For God so loved the world that He gave His only begotten Son, that whoever believes in Him should not perish but have everlasting life."* As born-again believers, His Spirit in us is influencing us and imploring us to give. By His grace, God's giving heart is reflected in our lives.

We should always look on our giving as sowing a seed. I've heard it said this way, "Give as a seed that you sow and not as a debt that you owe." Jesus paid our debts to God with the sacrifice of Himself on the cross. His last words from the cross as recorded by John were, *"It is finished"* (John 19:25). Those same words in the Greek have been found on papyrus receipts excavated from the time of Christ. They indicate that a bill has been "paid in full." Jesus by His suffering and dying on the cross has paid in full all of the debts owed by us to our heavenly Father. Trying to pay those debts ourselves with our giving takes us out of the realm of grace and into the realm of legalism. When we give, we are not paying a debt, and we are not buying from God. We are sowing a seed into the soil of His kingdom, and we are expecting to reap a harvest. He even supplies the seed that we sow!

Our giving is not drudgery. It is the grace of God manifesting itself in our lives. Paul in 2 Corinthians 9:6-15 beautifully describes the joy of sowing into God's kingdom and helps us to understand that the grace of giving is a big part of the garden of paradise that Christ has brought to our hearts and lives:

6 But this I say: He who sows sparingly will also reap sparingly, and he who sows bountifully will also reap bountifully. 7 So let each one give as he purposes in his heart, not grudgingly or of necessity; for God loves a cheerful giver. 8 And God is able to make all grace abound toward you, that you, always having all sufficiency in all things, may have an abundance for every good work. 9 As it is written: "He has dispersed abroad, He has given to the poor; His righteousness endures forever." 10 Now may He who supplies seed to the sower, and bread for food, supply and multiply the seed you have sown and increase the fruits of your righteousness, 11 while you are enriched in everything for all liberality, which causes thanksgiving through us to God. 12 For the administration of this service not only supplies the needs of the saints, but also is abounding through many thanksgivings to God, 13 while, through the proof of this ministry, they glorify God for the obedience of your confession to the gospel of Christ, and for your liberal sharing with them and all men, 14 and by their prayer for you, who long for you because of the exceeding grace of God in you. 15 Thanks be to God for His indescribable gift!

Again, we see the word "grace" featured prominently in Paul's exhortation to the Corinthians regarding giving. In verse 8 we see that grace originates with God and abounds toward us. In verses 14 and 15 grace is "exceeding" (beyond

our imaginations) and is a gift from God that is so wonderful
we really cannot adequately describe it.

During my lifetime, I have noticed that, as these verses indicate, generous givers are happy, cheerful people. The stingy
usually appear to be miserable. Givers are not resisting the
operation of God's grace in their lives. The garden of paradise
that God has placed in our hearts thrives and grows when we
cheerfully sow the seed that He has given us. This is exciting
when we remember that paradise's grace operates according
to agricultural principles and produces yields according to the
mathematics of grace described in the previous chapter of this
book.

In verse 8, Paul identifies two of the results of God's
abounding grace operating in the garden of the cheerful giver's life: (1) personal needs met, and (2) abundance for sowing
into every good (Spirit-led) work. In order to avoid legalism,
it is good to remember here that it is grace for works and not
works for grace. Grace always comes to us on the basis of the
merits of Jesus and His works rather than on our own personal
merits. The seeds we sow are provided by God because of the
redemptive work of Jesus on the cross.

Just as a farmer holds back some of his harvest for personal needs, so God expects us to provide for ourselves and our
families. If we will allow His abounding grace to direct our
sowing of the seed that He gives us, we will find that the harvest is plentiful enough to meet our needs and to continue to
sow bountifully into His work on the earth today. The above
text (verses 9-10) also emphasizes that God is the one Who
provides the seeds that we have available for personal needs
and for sowing into His kingdom.

He has given us a powerful seed spreader which sows to the
needs of the poor and also reaches *"abroad"* (verse 9). Abroad
means to other nations. When we sow seeds of financial sup-

port to the poor and to ministries in other countries, I believe with all my heart that many of the recipients will do exactly as Paul describes in the above text. They will give thanks to God for you and will pray for you with sincerity of heart, *"longing for you because of the exceeding grace of God in you."* Paul refers to this kind of prayer as *"God's indescribable gift."*

In 2005, I wrote the lyrics to a song entitled "Over the Sea," which expresses how powerful intercessory prayer can spring up from sowing into world missions:

Over the Sea

Verse 1

**I know that somewhere over the sea
There's someone kneeling and praying for me
I may not ever meet them here
But I know them in my heart
They're interceding in the Holy Spirit
They're offering the perfect prayer for me
I don't even know the language they speak
But I know they're in the gap for me**

Verse 2

**I know that somewhere over the sea
There's someone needing a prayer from me
I may not ever meet them here
But I know them in my heart
I'm interceding in the Holy Spirit
I'm offering the perfect prayer for them
They don't even know the language I speak
But I know I'm in the gap for them**

Chorus

Over the sea, over the sea
I know there's someone praying for me
Over the sea, over the sea
I know there's someone on their knees for me
Over the sea, over the sea
I know there's someone praying for me
Over the sea, over the sea
I know there's someone giving thanks for me[11]

There's something about giving and receiving that imparts the motivation to pray. If we are on the receiving end, there's that supernatural motivation to pray for the giver. If we are on the giving end, our prayers seem to always go with our gifts. This is because the gift is part of God's grace and carries His divine influence and blessing. It is as though every offering is gift-wrapped in prayer!

Not only does our church regularly pray for the ministries we support, I know from my conversations and visits to other countries that the churches and believers there pray fervently for those who sow into the work God is doing through them. And I mean they really pray! Because of the time zones, some countries are awake while we are asleep and vice versa. Taking part in the Great Commission (Matthew 28:18-20) by sowing financial seeds into world missions places the giver in the middle of a 24/7 intercessory prayer meeting. It is very comforting to know that while we sleep, there are precious prayer warriors interceding and thanking God for us! Only in eternity will we completely understand the magnitude of this great Spirit-led prayer meeting. It truly is *"God's indescribable gift!"*

There is much debate and argument over whether the tithe should be part of New Testament giving. Those who argue against tithing usually say that it is part of the Old Testament law and is not required by the New Testament. Certainly, tithing is not a condition for salvation. There is only one thing required to be saved and that is to accept Jesus Christ as one's personal Lord and Savior. No one is over a sincere decision away from having a personal relationship with God. However, we do see the principle of tithing being practiced in the Bible by Abraham and his descendants during the patriarchal age (Genesis 14:20, 28:22) before the giving of the Levitical law to Moses. Also, we find tithing being encouraged and taught in Old Testament verses that point to the Messianic age. Finally, some of the strongest teaching on tithing is found in the Book of Hebrews in the New Testament. In general, the tithe is the first ten percent of one's increase. Again, we should look on all of our giving, including the tithe, as a seed that we sow and not as a debt that we owe. When we give our tithes, we are not buying or earning from God; we are sowing a seed. The principle of tithing teaches us to sow the first and best part of our increase into the kingdom of God. Tithing fits beautifully within "Grace Like a Garden!"

The main theme of Hebrews chapter 7 is the changing of the priesthood. Hebrews 7:12-14 states that Jesus Christ, the high priest of the New Covenant is from a different tribe (Judah) than the high priest in the Mosaic Covenant who was always from the tribe of Levi: *For the priesthood being changed, of necessity there is also a change of the law. For He of whom these things are spoken belongs to another tribe, from which no man has officiated at the altar. For it is evident that our Lord arose from Judah, of which tribe Moses spoke nothing concerning priesthood.*

Hebrews also makes it clear that unlike the Old Covenant, the high priest of the New Covenant will remain our high priest forever because of His endless life. The author of Hebrews brings this truth home by comparing Jesus to a man named Melchizedek who was king of Salem and *"priest of the Most High God"* during the time of Abraham (7:1). Hebrews 7:15-17 clearly shows that this Melchizedek was a type and foreshadow of our high priest and king, Jesus Christ: *And it is yet far more evident if, in the likeness of Melchizedek, there arises another priest who has come, not according to the law of a fleshly commandment, but according to the power of an endless life. For He testifies: "You are a priest forever according to the order of Melchizedek."* Hebrews 7:1-3 also compares Melchizedek to the *"Son of God"* (Jesus): *For this Melchizedek, king of Salem, priest of the Most High God, who met Abraham returning from the slaughter of the kings and blessed him, to whom also Abraham gave a tenth part of all, first being translated "king of righteousness," and then also king of Salem, meaning "king of peace," without genealogy, having neither beginning of days nor end of life, but made like the Son of God, remains a priest continually.*

Abraham lived long before the giving of the Levitical law to Moses, and yet the above text records his having given a tithe to Melchizedek. This is of great significance when we realize that Abraham was actually a product of the gospel which was preached to him. Galatians 3:5-9 confirms that Abraham was a type and foreshadow of the Christian who receives righteousness by faith rather than by the works of the law: *Therefore He who supplies the Spirit to you and works miracles among you, does He do it by the works of the law, or by the hearing of faith? – just as Abraham "believed God, and it was accounted to him for righteousness." Therefore know that only those who are of faith are sons of Abraham. And the Scripture, foreseeing that God would justify the Gentiles by faith, preached the gospel to Abraham beforehand, saying "In you all the nations shall be blessed." So then those who are of faith are blessed with believing Abraham.*

As we read in Hebrews 7, Abraham, who is a type and foreshadow of the New Testament believer, gave a tithe to Melchizedek, who is a type and foreshadow of our high priest Jesus Christ. At that time, there was no written law requiring Abraham to tithe to Melchizedek. Abraham tithed to Melchizedek because of the divine influence in his heart. His tithe was not motivated by a written law but by grace.

Hebrews 7:8 speaks of the present time: *Here mortal men receive tithes, but there he receives them, of whom it is witnessed that he lives.* Here mortal men, leaders in the church, have stewardship over the tithes we give, but Jesus Christ, our High Priest, is receiving them in His heart. Hebrews 8:1-2 gives a summary conclusion of Hebrews chapter 7: *Now this is the main point of the things we are saying: We have such a High Priest, who is seated at the right hand of the throne of the Majesty in the heavens, a Minister of the sanctuary and of the true tabernacle which the Lord erected, and not man.* The tithe is something so precious that, spiritually speaking, it goes straight to the throne of God.

Malachi is the last book in the Old Testament. Its third chapter gives a direct reference to John the Baptist and to the Messiah Jesus in its very first verse: *"Behold, I send My messenger, and he will prepare the way before Me. And the Lord, whom you seek, will suddenly come to His temple, even the Messenger of the covenant, in whom I delight. Behold, He is coming,"* *says the LORD of hosts.* In Matthew 11:10 Jesus confirms that Malachi was speaking prophetically of John the Baptist and of Himself: *For this is he of whom it is written: "Behold, I send My messenger before Your face, who will prepare Your way before You."* We can conclude from this that Malachi chapter 3 points to the Messianic age and the New Covenant.

Interestingly, Malachi 3:10-12 also gives a very powerful teaching on the tithe: *10 "Bring all the tithes into the* *storehouse, That there may be food in My house, And try Me now in this," Says the Lord of hosts, "If I will not open for you the windows of heaven And pour out for you such blessing That there will not be room enough to receive it. **11** "And I will rebuke the devourer for your sakes, So that he will not destroy the fruit of your ground, Nor shall the vine fail to bear fruit for you in the field," Says the Lord of hosts; **12** "And all nations will call you blessed, For you will be a delightful land," Says the Lord of hosts.*

Once again, we see how God has an agricultural view of our giving. When we tithe, we are sowing a seed in God's kingdom. The tithe fits beautifully within the theme of "Grace Like a Garden." The tithe produces crops according to God's agricultural principles of sowing and reaping and is inspired by the divine influence of Jesus in the garden of our hearts.

The tithe provides for the expenses and operation of the local church, *"that there may be food in My house."* Many years ago, my wife and I were asked to speak at a church conference near Mexico City. The churches represented the oldest Pentecostal denomination in Mexico. One of the largest churches was made up of thousands of indigenous people. They were of very small stature, but they were big in heart. They were from a remote area of southern Mexico that was virtually cut off from the rest of the country. They even had their own language and did not speak Spanish like the rest of Mexico. Their local economy was agricultural and was based entirely on the barter system. They did not use currency. At their church they actually had storage facilities for grain, livestock, and other agricultural products that were brought in by the members as tithes and offerings. Their church literally was *"the storehouse!"*

At one of the meetings, these precious believers actually pleaded with their denomination to let them host the next year's conference. They gave a report on how many cows, turkeys, bushels of grain, and other produce they had already stored at their church in anticipation of being the host. The other churches' hearts melted, and they enthusiastically agreed to let them host. We were thrilled to vividly see a modern-day illustration of the beautiful agricultural nature of God's grace in giving.

While most of us do not have farms, we do have salaries and/or other sources of income. And while most of us do not have barns, we do have bank accounts and/or other investments. We can apply Malachi's agricultural principles of tithing by sowing the first ten percent of our incomes into our local churches. When we pour in, God pours out. According to the above verses, the harvest manifests in open windows of heaven (v.10), overflowing blessing (v.10), rebuke of the devourer and destroyer (v.11), guaranteed fruit (v.11), and a favorable and attractive witness to a lost and hurting world (v.12). All of this is very exciting when we realize that tithing is very fair to all. It's based on percentage rather than on absolute amount. For example, a tithe of $3,000 on an income of $30,000 is just as powerful a seed as a tithe of $100,000 on an income of $1,000,000.

Windows can be looked out from, and also, they provide a look in. Understanding that God is omniscient (all-knowing) makes open windows of heaven (v.10) an extremely valuable asset for the believer. One of the ways God can pour out a blessing is by giving the believer supernatural information. He gives the believer a look into His window regarding the future. I have personally experienced this regarding investments. Inside information for profit in the corporate world can be corrupt and dishonest, but information from God is a holy and honest blessing! This information can come through a dream, a vision, a prophetic word, or simply through the still small voice of the Holy Spirit. How exciting it is to realize that

God's windows are open for us! The open window of heaven could be direction regarding a career opportunity. It could be a word of wisdom or a word of knowledge (1 Corinthians 9:8) regarding something that brings a blessing to your employer and a promotion for you. It could be an idea for a new invention that blesses humanity and brings royalties to you.

The overflowing blessing promised as part of the tithe's harvest in v.10 puts the believer in position to give above tithe offerings which continue to produce multiplied harvest. With the tithe, God places a key in our hands that opens the doorway to the manifestations of the mathematics of grace in our finances! The tithe is also like a weed killer and spiritual insecticide that prevents the enemy from destroying and devouring the harvest from our offerings (v.11). It's an insurance policy and guarantee regarding the fruit from the garden of grace that God has placed in our hearts (v.11). And most importantly, our lives and witness become more attractive to a lost and hurting world. The gardens of our lives become a *"delightful land"* (v.12) that draws the attention of the observer whose heart is considering eternity. They begin to see the paradise in you.

There is another principle of sowing that, like the tithe, teaches us to sow the first and best part of our increase into the soil of God's kingdom. It is the offering of firstfruits. The Israelis would take the first ripened part of their harvest and offer it to God. Sometimes believers today will flow in the spirit of the firstfruits offering by bringing into the church the first paycheck of a new job or of a promoted position. Another way of sowing firstfruits could be giving the first revenue check of a new investment to the Lord by sowing it into Christian ministry. In my opinion, these modern-day versions of the giving of firstfruits should be done only as the Holy Spirit leads, knowing that it is He Who brings forth the harvest. Proverbs 3:9-10 describes the harvest that results from the Spirit-led giving of firstfruits: *Honor the LORD with your possessions, and with the firstfruits of all your increase; so your barns will be filled with plenty and your vats will overflow with new wine.* This agricultural principle of sowing and reaping also fits beautifully into our title of "Grace Like a Garden." As with the tithe, you may not have a barn or a wine vat, but you probably have a bank account and/or other investment accounts. I believe that the wine points to the blood bought promises of the New Covenant. It's all about His grace. It's all about Jesus! Only because of His sacrifice are we given the privilege of sowing the fristfruits into His kingdom. 1 Corinthians 15:20 even refers to the risen Christ as the firstfruits: *But now Christ is risen from the dead, and has become the firstfruits of those who have fallen asleep.* When the believer sows a firstfruits offering, it is good to thank Jesus for His resurrection power flowing in his finances. It is Jesus Who raised up that new job! It is Jesus Who provided that pay raise. With the firstfruits offering, we should always give glory to Christ and His resurrection power!

Another area of grace in giving is the sowing of alms, which includes giving to the poor and those in need. This area of flowing in God's grace is especially warming to the heart and helps keep the soil of our spiritual gardens at the right temperature for germination of all the seeds we have sown. When we have mercy on the poor, God's loving grace is flowing through us. Proverbs 19:17 assures us that the Lord will see to it that we will reap a harvest in kind: *He who has pity on the poor lends to the LORD, and He will pay back what he has given.* Think about this Scripture. When we sow pity or compassion by helping the poor, God's compassion, like sunlight, nourishes the gardens of our lives and brings forth abundant harvests! Paradise loves mercy!

One area of grace in giving that we must not leave out is that of extending mercy to our enemies. God's Word says, *"If your enemy is hungry, give him bread to eat; and if he is thirsty, give him water to drink; for so you will heap coals of fire on his head, and the LORD will reward you"* (Proverbs 25:21-22). It was customary in the culture of the Middle East to wrap hot coals in animal skins or fabric and place them on one's head as a way to stay warm in very cold weather. The mistake that believers sometimes make regarding this area of giving is that they look to that same enemy for their harvest, but the above scripture tells us that the reward comes from the Lord and not from the person who was helped. God's field of harvest is immense. His rain, sunshine, and nourishment can produce growth and fruit all over the garden of your life! It may be that the seed you plant in that contrary person's heart and life will eventually soften and melt their hardness and bring them to the place of repentance, but even if it doesn't, your reward is sure.

In Matthew 5:43-48, Jesus clearly gives us instruction regarding our enemies: *43 "You have heard that it was said, 'You shall love your neighbor and hate your enemy.' 44 But I say to you, love your enemies, bless those who curse you, do good to those who hate you, and pray for those who spitefully use you and persecute you, 45 that you may be sons of your Father in heaven; for He makes His sun rise on the evil and on the good, and sends rain on the just and on the unjust. 46 For if you love those who love you, what reward have you? Do not even the tax collectors do the same? 47 And if you greet your brethren only, what do you do more than others? Do not even the tax collectors do so? 48 Therefore you shall be perfect, just as your Father in heaven is perfect."*

Your sowing of grace to your enemy when he is in need brings the warmth of God's presence and the refreshing well of His Spirit to your enemy, and your reward is certain. It is the light of His presence and the rain of His Spirit on the garden of your life! It's up to your enemy to acknowledge God, but you, who already know Him, receive and benefit from the blessing He pours out on you. Loving one's enemy is a sign of a mature believer.

Galatians 6:6-10 concerns sowing into Christian ministry and gives assurance of a harvest: *6 Let him who is taught the word share in all good things with him who teaches. 7 Do not be deceived, God is not mocked; for whatever a man sows, that he will also reap. 8 For he who sows to his flesh will of the flesh reap corruption, but he who sows to the Spirit will of the Spirit reap everlasting life. 9 And let us not grow weary while doing good, for in due season we shall reap if we do not lose heart. 10 Therefore, as we have opportunity, let us do good to all, especially to those who are of the household of faith.*

God does not want us to be deceived. When we hear the world, and even some in the church, mocking the principle of sowing and reaping, we need to be careful not to enter into that flow of deception. A favorite excuse of the unbelieving world is "preachers only want your money." Before my salvation and deliverance from alcohol many years ago, I remember sitting at a bar one evening when the discussion of churches and preachers surfaced. The bartender said, "All they want is your money." Others, including me, joined in agreement. Of course, we were all doling out the money for our drinks. Before I left that evening, I gave a big tip to the bartender and paid for a round of drinks for the others at the bar.

In Psalm 69:12, David said, *"Those who sit in the gate speak against me, and I am the song of the drunkards."* That night in the bar, I and the others were singing *"the song of the drunkards."* Now as a believer and a preacher, I refuse to be deceived. I will not mock God. When we sow His seed, we are sowing to the Spirit. The spiritual motion of sowing is beautiful and is actually an act of worship. Sowing to the Spirit is holy and should never be ridiculed. King David said, *"Bring*

an offering and come before Him, Oh worship the LORD in the beauty of holiness" (1 Chronicles 16:29b)!
Of course, there are always some who will lack integrity in the handling of money. Those unfortunate situations should be dealt with soberly by the church. Generalizing is very dangerous. Even well-meaning people can be deceived into jumping on the bandwagon of a judgmental and critical spirit. We must be careful not to sing with the drunkards! If we do, we could find ourselves opposed to God Himself! The principle of sowing and reaping is real. It is holy. It functions in His garden of grace. His Word is true!

Whether our sowing is that of an offering, a tithe, first fruits, alms, or mercy to an enemy, the harvest is guaranteed. *"Whatever a man sows, that he will also reap"* (Galatians 6:7). The harvest will be in kind. If we sow money, we will reap financially. Whatever we sow, that is what we will reap. Try smiling at someone in the grocery store. Most of the time that person will immediately smile back. There is an immediate harvest in kind. It is very important that we sow to the spirit rather than to the flesh. Sow hatred toward someone, and that person will likely hate you in return. Grace flows with love rather than with hatred. God gives us the seed to sow. When we sow His seed, we are sowing to the Spirit.

The deceiver, the devil, also makes seed available to humanity. His seeds are at enmity with God and include selfishness, jealousy, lust, pride, dishonesty, racism, rebellion, and the like. The choice is ours. We can sow to the Spirit, or we can sow to the flesh (the weakness of our humanity).

When we follow the Holy Spirit and the Word of God with our giving, we are flowing in that divine influence of grace. We are sowing to the Spirit. The harvest is guaranteed, but it is not always immediate (Galatians 6:9). The timing of the harvest is referred to as *"in due season."* Praise God! There is a "due season!" The harvest will come! Don't give up! "Do not lose heart!" Your "due season" could be nearer than you think!

Regular, steady giving to your church and to Christian ministry is a good plan because you always have seed in the ground. You can look forward to many due seasons of harvest because you are always sowing.

I offer the following prayer to help you commit to grace in giving:

Father God, I thank you for giving me seed to sow. I declare that You are my source. I am determined to flow in the divine influence of your grace with my giving as I follow the Holy Spirit and Your Word for direction. Help me to see myself as a farmer in paradise rather than a banker in the world. May every seed I sow find its due season of harvest in the garden of my life. Thank You for opening the windows of heaven for me. May my eyes be opened to see the good soil before me. Give me the courage to see the merits of Jesus Christ as my strength in the fields of my life. In those times of waiting when the plants have yet to break through the surface, give me the patience of hope for divine germination. When the joy of the harvest comes, give me the presence to offer praise and glory to You! In the name of Jesus, amen.

Chapter 7

Watering Your Garden

Any garden needs water in order to be healthy and to grow. Without water, the soil dries, and the plants thirst to death. Following is a quote by gardening expert Monique Allen regarding the importance of water for plants: "It is almost impossible to overestimate the importance of water for your garden – after all, water makes up 85 to 95 percent of the weight of living plants. In fact, plants use more water than anything else. Water carries nutrients from the soil to the plant cells, so plants that are kept at their desired hydration level will be stronger and healthier."[12]

Like natural gardens, the gardens of our lives need spiritual water to be strong and healthy. That spiritual water comes to us through the Holy Spirit and the Word of God. God provided a river to water the Garden of Eden: *"Now a river went out of Eden to water the garden, and from there it parted and became four riverheads"* (Genesis 2:10).

God also has provided the river of the Holy Spirit to water the garden of paradise in our hearts, and to flow forth from us to impact the lives of others. Jesus declared in John 7:37-39: *37 On the last day, that great day of the feast, Jesus stood and cried out, saying, "If anyone thirsts, let him come to Me and drink. 38 He who believes in Me, as the Scripture has said, out of his heart will flow rivers of living water." 39 But this He spoke concerning the Spirit, whom those believing in Him would receive; for the Holy Spirit was not yet given, because Jesus was not yet glorified.*

When one accepts Jesus Christ as his or her personal Lord and Savior, that person is regenerated by and receives an ever-abiding presence of the Holy Spirit. This happens at the time of the new birth. God also wants us to be filled to overflowing with the Holy Spirit. Through Jesus Christ, the Holy Spirit (the river of God) is poured out abundantly for all those who will receive. We can not earn the Holy Spirit by our works. His presence and outpouring are available because of grace, the unmerited mercy that comes to us through Jesus Christ and the merits of His works at Calvary. As Titus 3:4-7 explains, Jesus loves us and wants us to have the full flow of the river of the Holy Spirit in the gardens of our lives: *4 But when the kindness and the love of God our Savior toward man appeared, 5 not by works of righteousness which we have done, but according to His mercy He saved us, through the washing of regeneration and renewing of the Holy Spirit, 6 whom He poured out on us abundantly through Jesus Christ our Savior; 7 that having been justified by His grace we should become heirs according to the hope of eternal life.*

The waters of God are free and available to everyone who believes. Isaiah beautifully expresses God's invitation of grace: *"Ho! Everyone who thirsts, come to the waters; and you who have no money, come, buy and eat. Yes, come, buy wine and milk without money and without price"* (Isaiah 55:1). We can't pay for the waters of God because the price has already been paid by the precious blood of our Lord and Savior Jesus Christ. In the above verse, I believe the milk points to the Word of God, and the wine points to the Holy Spirit. In the New Testament, Peter wrote, *"As newborn babes, desire the pure milk of the word, that you may grow thereby, if indeed you have tasted that the Lord is gracious"* (1 Peter 2:2-3). Concerning wine, Paul wrote, *"And do not be drunk with wine, in which is dissipation, but be filled with the Spirit"* (Ephesians 5:18).

I will never forget my experience of being baptized in the Holy Spirit. I had been born again a week earlier and wanted everything that God had for me. As believers laid hands on me in the name of Jesus, I began to speak in a language different from English. It was a language that no one had taught me. I was overcome by the Holy Spirit and actually fell on the floor. I was drunk with the new wine of the Holy Spirit. It was the most wonderful feeling I had ever had in my life! For several minutes, I could hardly walk. I realized that my past addictions to alcohol and drugs had simply been counterfeits that the devil offers fallen humanity. I was now experiencing the real thing!

It's interesting that the first miracle by Jesus recorded in the New Testament was His turning the water into wine at the wedding in Cana. That first miracle paralleled the turning of the water into blood by Moses in the Old Testament and pointed to Jesus as the Messiah. It was also looking forward to believers leaving behind the drunkenness of the wine of this world and being filled with the new wine of the Holy Spirit! I have been free of alcohol and drugs for over thirty-six years now. I don't need them. I am on the new wine of the Holy Spirit!

The Book of Acts gives a history of the early years of the church. Several chapters give descriptions of believers being baptized in the Holy Spirit, which is also referred to as being filled with the Holy Spirit. Jesus had told those who were there at Mount Olivet when He ascended that they would be baptized with the Holy Spirit not many days from then: *And being assembled together with them, He commanded them not to depart from Jerusalem, but to wait for the Promise of the Father, "which," He said, "You have heard from Me; for John truly baptized with water, but you shall be baptized with the Holy Spirit not many days from now"* (Acts 1:4-5). In John 20:22 Jesus, after His resurrection and before His ascension, *"breathed on them, and said to them, "Receive the Holy Spirit."* Those same disciples who had received the Holy Spirit in regeneration measure were now to wait for the promised baptismal measure of the same Holy Spirit.

Acts 2:1-13 gives account of their experience of being baptized in the Holy Spirit (referred to here as being *"filled with the Holy Spirit"*) and the crowd's response: *1 When the Day of Pentecost had fully come, they were all with one accord in one place. 2 And suddenly there came a sound from heaven, as of a rushing mighty wind, and it filled the whole house where they were sitting. 3 Then there appeared to them divided tongues, as of fire, and one sat upon each of them. 4 And they were all filled with the Holy Spirit and began to speak with other tongues, as the Spirit gave them utterance. 5 And there were dwelling in Jerusalem Jews, devout men, from every nation under heaven. 6 And when this sound occurred, the multitude came together, and were confused, because everyone heard them speak in his own language. 7 Then they were all amazed and marveled, saying to one another, "Look, are not all these who speak Galileans? 8 And how is it that we hear, each in our own language in which we were born? 9 Parthians and Medes and Elamites, those dwelling in Mesopotamia, Judea and Cappadocia, Pontus and Asia, 10 Phrygia and Pamphylia, Egypt and the parts of Libya adjoining Cyrene, visitors from Rome, both Jews and proselytes, 11 Cretans and Arabs--we hear them speaking in our own tongues the wonderful works of God." 12 So they were all amazed and perplexed, saying to one another, "Whatever could this mean?" 13 Others mocking said, "They are full of new wine."*

The Holy Spirit announced His arrival with the sound of a rushing mighty wind. There were visible manifestations of tongues of fire upon the believers. They also spoke in other tongues, languages that they had not been taught. These were spontaneous languages that were given to them by the Holy Spirit. They appeared to the onlookers to be drunk on wine.

Peter began to preach to the crowd that had gathered. He started out by clarifying that the disciples were not drunk on the wine of this world. Peter continued his message by quoting from the prophet Joel and went on to explain to the crowd that they had witnessed an outpouring of the Holy Spirit by Jesus Himself: *"This Jesus God has raised up, of which we are all witnesses. Therefore being exalted to the right hand of God, and having received from the Father the promise of the Holy Spirit, He has poured out this which you now see and hear"* (Acts 2:32-33). About three thousand onlookers were saved and added to the church after Peter's preaching that day (Acts 2:41).

Nearly always there are those who will mock at those who experience the baptism in the Holy Spirit. They were there on the Day of Pentecost, and they are around today. They especially seem to get upset by the manifestation of speaking in tongues. However, Acts chapter two is not the only place in the Scriptures that endorses speaking in tongues. Peter was sent on a divine mission to preach the Gospel to the Gentiles at the household of a centurion named Cornelius who lived in Caesarea. Acts 10:44-47 records that those with Cornelius spoke with tongues when the Holy Spirit was poured out on them: *44 While Peter was still speaking these words, the Holy Spirit fell upon all those who heard the word. 45 And those of the circumcision who believed were astonished, as many as came with Peter, because the gift of the Holy Spirit had been poured out on the Gentiles also. 46 For they heard them speak with tongues and magnify God. Then Peter answered, 47 "Can anyone forbid water, that these should not be baptized who have received the Holy Spirit just as we have?"* Like those in Acts 2, believers in Acts 10 spoke in tongues and magnified God when they were filled with the Holy Spirit.

Acts 19:1-7 records Paul's ministering to some disciples of John the Baptist at Ephesus: *1 And it happened, while Apollos was at Corinth, that Paul, having passed through the upper regions, came to Ephesus. And finding some disciples 2 he said to them, "Did you receive the Holy Spirit when you believed?" So they said to him, "We have not so much as heard whether there is a Holy Spirit." 3 And he said to them, "Into what then were you baptized?" So they said, "Into John's baptism." 4 Then Paul said, "John indeed baptized with a baptism of repentance, saying to the people that they should believe on Him who would come after him, that is, on Christ Jesus." 5 When they heard this, they were baptized in the name of the Lord Jesus. 6 And when Paul had laid hands on them, the Holy Spirit came upon them, and they spoke with tongues and prophesied. 7 Now the men were about twelve in all.* Paul acknowledged that these twelve men were already believers, and it is obvious from the above text that his question to them concerned being filled with the Holy Spirit. Otherwise, he would not have baptized them in water because water baptism is clearly for believers only. Here, as in Acts 2 and Acts 10, we see the experience of being filled with the Holy Spirit accompanied by speaking in tongues. During the next two years, Paul reached all of Asia Minor with the Gospel of Jesus Christ with this team of twelve Spirit-filled believers (Acts 19:10).

In 1 Corinthians 12:10, speaking in "different kinds of tongues" is listed as a valid gift of the Holy Spirit. In 1 Corinthians chapter 14, Paul gives in-depth teaching and instruction regarding use of this gift, especially in public meetings. He closes the chapter with *"Therefore brethren, desire earnestly to prophesy, and do not forbid to speak with tongues. Let all things be done decently and in order"* (1 Corinthians 14:39-40). Paul discusses both praying in tongues and giving messages in tongues in 1 Corinthians chapter 14. When a message in a tongue is given in a public meeting, there should be an interpretation of the tongue so that those gathered can be edified. The interpretation of tongues is also a valid gift of the Holy Spirit listed in 1 Corinthians 12:10. The tongue may be interpreted by the person giving it or by someone else in the meeting. I have written a little book entitled <u>Hot Line from God</u>[13] which takes the reader through 1 Corinthians 14 in detail. It is available at our online bookstore <u>www.battleministries.com</u>.

As I shared above, I began to speak in a language that no one had taught me when I was filled with the Holy Spirit. Since that time, I have continued to pray in this language every day and have become more fluent with it. One of the greatest blessings of my life has been the gift of this personal prayer language, and I encourage all believers to ask God for this blessing. In reference to praying in tongues, Paul wrote, *"He who speaks in a tongue edifies himself"* (1 Corinthians 14:4a). When a person prays in tongues, his or her inner person is being recharged with the Holy Spirit in much the same way that batteries are recharged. Most of the time when I pray in tongues, I do not receive an interpretation, but my spirit is being built up or edified. Jude wrote the following, *"But you, beloved, building yourselves up on your most holy faith, praying in the Holy Spirit, keep yourselves in the love of God, looking for the mercy of our Lord Jesus Christ unto eternal life"* (Jude 20-21). *"Praying in the Holy Spirit"* in this verse is probably a reference to praying in tongues, which Paul referred to as praying with the spirit (1 Corinthians 14:14-15).

Going back to that beautiful gazebo in the center of the garden of grace that God has placed in our hearts, it is a wonderful blessing to include praying in tongues as part of our meeting with Him there. It's like turning on a divine sprinkler system which brings the needed water of the Spirit to the gardens of our lives. Have you ever seen a rainbow appear across the spray of a sprinkling system? It's a beautiful sight. The rainbow was the sign of God's covenant with Noah. When we sit in the presence of God praying in the Spirit, we are exhibiting a sign of our covenant as believers in Jesus Christ. Jesus included speaking in tongues as one of the signs of a believer: *"And these signs will follow those who believe: In My name they will cast out demons; they will speak with new tongues"* (Mark 16:17). This sign not only includes public messages in other tongues; it includes praying and worshipping in our prayer languages as we meet with God in our gardens of grace.

One should never be afraid to ask God for more of the Holy Spirit. Jesus said: *"If a son asks for bread from any father among you, will he give him a stone? Or if he asks for a fish, will he give him a serpent instead of a fish? Or if he asks for an egg, will he offer him a scorpion? If you then, being evil, know how to give good gifts to your children, how much more will your heavenly Father give the Holy Spirit to those who ask Him!"* (Luke 11:11-13). We should not be intimidated by man-made theology. The baptism in the Holy Spirit, along with speaking in tongues, is clearly encouraged by the Scriptures and has been available to every generation since Acts chapter two.

The Bible also likens the Word of God to water. The Scriptures provide both seeds and water for the paradise of grace in our hearts. In Ephesians 5:25-29, Paul describes the Word of God as spiritual water that the husband uses to wash, nourish, and cherish his wife in the same way that Christ does the church: *25 Husbands, love your wives, just as Christ also loved the church and gave Himself for her, 26 that He might sanctify and cleanse her with the washing of water by the word, 27 that He might present her to Himself a glorious church, not having spot or wrinkle or any such thing, but that she should be holy and without blemish. 28 So husbands ought to love their own wives as their own bodies; he who loves his wife loves himself. 29 For no one ever hated his own flesh, but nourishes and cherishes it, just as the Lord does the church.*

One of my favorite times of the day is morning. My wife Schar and I love to sit in our living room and read our Bibles and pray. The Holy Spirit is always there with us to teach us from God's textbook, the Bible. When the Holy Spirit breathes on a scripture and brings it alive for me, I will often share His blessing with Schar, and she does the same for me. When this happens, we are, in essence, washing each other with the water of God's Word. Washing with the water of the Word is not an abrasive action but rather one of tenderness. It is a way of cherishing one another. It is a way of expressing the love of Jesus to one another. Jesus pours His love into the marriage with the water of His Word.

Whether with one's spouse or alone with God, reading and meditating on the Word of God opens the heart to God's irrigation system. Psalm 1:2-3 describes the results of meditating on the Word of God: *2 But his delight is in the law of the Lord, And in His law he meditates day and night. 3 He shall be like a tree Planted by the rivers of water, That brings forth its fruit in its season, Whose leaf also shall not wither; And whatever he does shall prosper.* Clearly, these verses link a healthy spiritual garden with the rivers of water provided by the Word of God. Daily reading, meditating on, and digesting the Scriptures ensure the health of God's plants in our lives and guarantee that the fruit of our harvests will be prosperous and on time.

God also uses our tears to water the garden of grace that He has placed in our hearts. Tears of repentance, brokenness, and compassion are precious to the Lord. David describes the importance of tears in Psalm 56:8-9: *You number my wanderings; Put my tears into Your bottle; Are they not in Your book? When I cry out to You, Then my enemies will turn back; This I know, because God is for me.* Charles Spurgeon said, "When you are so weak that you cannot do much more than cry, you coin diamonds with both your eyes. The sweetest prayers God ever hears are the groans and sighs of those who have no hope in anything but His love."[14]

These tears often come just before the breakthrough of resurrection power, and they are sometimes accompanied by groanings because the intercession is so powerful that words cannot adequately express what is going on in the heart. This type of spiritual, intercessory prayer is described in Romans 8:26-27: *Likewise the Spirit also helps in our weaknesses. For we do not know what we should pray for as we ought, but the Spirit Himself makes intercession for us with groanings which cannot be uttered. Now He who searches the hearts knows what the mind of the Spirit is, because He makes intercession for the saints according to the will of God.*

We see the power of tears and groaning displayed in the ministry of Jesus Himself when He raised His friend Lazarus from the dead as recorded in John 11:32-44:

32 Then, when Mary came where Jesus was, and saw Him, she fell down at His feet, saying to Him, "Lord, if You had been here, my brother would not have died." 33 Therefore, when Jesus saw her weeping, and the Jews who came with her weeping, He groaned in the spirit and was troubled. 34 And He said, "Where have you laid him?" They said to Him, "Lord, come and see." 35 Jesus wept. 36 Then the Jews said, "See how He loved him!" 37 And some of them said, "Could not this

Man, who opened the eyes of the blind, also have kept this man from dying?" **38** *Then Jesus, again groaning in Himself, came to the tomb. It was a cave, and a stone lay against it.* **39** *Jesus said, "Take away the stone." Martha, the sister of him who was dead, said to Him, "Lord, by this time there is a stench, for he has been dead four days."* **40** *Jesus said to her, "Did I not say to you that if you would believe you would see the glory of God?"* **41** *Then they took away the stone from the place where the dead man was lying. And Jesus lifted up His eyes and said, "Father, I thank You that You have heard Me.* **42** *And I know that You always hear Me, but because of the people who are standing by I said this, that they may believe that You sent Me."* **43** *Now when He had said these things, He cried with a loud voice, "Lazarus, come forth!"* **44** *And he who had died came out bound hand and foot with graveclothes, and his face was wrapped with a cloth. Jesus said to them, "Loose him, and let him go."*

"Jesus wept" (v.35) is the shortest verse in the Bible, but it is also one of the most powerful verses. The tears and groanings of Jesus were followed by His command, *"Lazarus, come forth!"*

The purpose of prayer is not to change the will of God but, rather, to find the will of God and agree with it. In the Garden of Gethsemane, Jesus brought His will in agreement with the will of His Father that He would suffer and die on the cross for us. Hebrews 5:7 describes the prayer life of Jesus as including *"vehement cries and tears."* This kind of prayer is often prompted by death type situations in our lives and paves the way for the resurrection power of the Holy Spirit to take over. It might be the death of a marriage, career, ministry, budget, or dream one is facing. When we have done all we can do and take it to the cross with our tears, God sees and brings the grace of His resurrection power into that situation. His power may not always manifest in the way we are expecting, but we will recognize it when it happens. His ways are higher than our ways, and He is *"able to do exceedingly abundantly above all that we ask or think"* (Ephesians 3:20).

Psalm 126:5-6 gives a beautiful description of the ministry of tears in the garden of grace: *5 Those who sow in tears Shall reap in joy. 6 He who continually goes forth weeping, Bearing seed for sowing, Shall doubtless come again with rejoicing, Bringing his sheaves with him.*

In summary, the waters of God are always available to bring blessing and growth to the gardens of our lives. The river of God never runs dry! Psalm 65:9-10 promises: *9 You visit the earth and water it, You greatly enrich it; The river of God is full of water; You provide their grain, For so You have prepared it. 10 You water its ridges abundantly, You settle its furrows; You make it soft with showers, You bless its growth.*

I offer the following prayer to help you in your commitment to keep the garden of your life watered, healthy, and productive:

Dear Father in heaven, thank you for your grace. And I thank Your Son Jesus for paying the price for me to be able to come to the spiritual waters and drink freely. Thank You for the waters of Your Word and Your Holy Spirit. Give me a thirst for more of Your Word. Fill me to overflowing with the water of Your Spirit. Give me a new language with which to pray. Help me to see my tears as droplets of Your resurrection power. In the mighty name of Jesus, amen.

Chapter 8

Son Light for Your Garden

A ccording to author and agricultural expert Ivory Harlow, "Sunlight is the stuff plants crave. Plant growth and performance is fueled with energy from sunlight. Stationing your vegetable garden in a sunny spot ensures seedlings get the light they need to grow big and strong."[15] Just as a natural garden craves sunlight, the gardens of our hearts crave the light of the Son of God, Jesus Christ. We need His light to grow spiritually strong and healthy. When we surrendered our lives to Jesus, our hearts became paradises of grace. Eden needed light (Genesis 1:3). Our hearts need the light of Jesus.

The first chapter of the Gospel according to John includes "the Light" as one of the titles of Jesus: *1 In the beginning was the Word, and the Word was with God, and the Word was God. 2 He was in the beginning with God. 3 All things were made through Him, and without Him nothing was made that was made. 4 In Him was life, and the life was the light of men. 5 And the light shines in the darkness, and the darkness did not comprehend it. 6 There was a man sent from God, whose name was John. 7 This man came for a witness, to bear witness of the Light, that all through him might believe. 8 He was not that Light, but was sent to bear witness of that Light. 9 That was the true Light which gives light to every man coming into the world.*

The "true Light" is available to every person on earth. Jesus referred to Himself as "the light of the world" in John 8:12: *Then Jesus spoke to them again, saying, "I am the light of the world. He who follows Me shall not walk in darkness, but have the light of life."* When one accepts Jesus Christ as his or her personal Lord and Savior, that person receives the "light of life." When Jesus brings paradise to the heart of the believer, He brings His light with Him. Immediately, the believer should begin to see things differently.

Before surrendering to Christ, we all were often led by a false or counterfeit light. Paul even describes Satan as transforming himself into "an angel of light" (2 Corinthians 11:14). All of us, before coming to Christ, were led astray by this evil "prince of the power of the air," according Ephesians 2:1-3: *1 And you He made alive, who were dead in trespasses and sins, 2 in which you once walked according to the course of this world, according to the prince of the power of the air, the spirit who now works in the sons of disobedience, 3 among whom also we all once conducted ourselves in the lusts of our flesh, fulfilling the desires of the flesh and of the mind, and were by nature children of wrath, just as the others.*

But when we accepted Jesus Christ as our personal Lord and Savior, the "true Light" came into our hearts and lives. We began to recognize the lies and deceptions of the devil. Matthew described the impact of the earthly ministry of Jesus upon the region of Galilee by quoting from Isaiah's prophecy (Isaiah 9:1-2): *"The land of Zebulun and the land of Naphtali, By the way of the sea, beyond the Jordan, Galilee of the Gentiles: The people who sat in darkness have seen a great light, And upon those who sat in the region and shadow of death Light has dawned"* (Matthew 4:15-16). Before accepting Jesus Christ as our personal Lord and Savior, we were all like the inhabitants of Galilee, sitting in spiritual darkness. But when we surrendered our lives to the Savior, His light dawned in our hearts. His light can burn brighter and brighter if we will only surrender each day to His grace, which is His divine influence in our hearts. The light of the Son of God will cause the gardens of our lives to flourish and bear much fruit for His kingdom!

Before coming to Jesus with our lives, most of us had accumulated a lot of things which represent the counterfeits or false lights of that deceiver, the devil. Jesus referred to this spiritual enemy as a liar and the father of lies (John 8:44). It's good to throw the junk out of our surroundings when we have the authority to do so. This helps clear the soil and place the spiritual vegetation of our hearts in position to receive the true light of Christ.

My wife Schar and I had a library in our home that included some good books with a worldview that lined up with biblical moral values or at least did not oppose them. It also contained many books that were not good. We had not even read many of them. After our new births, we went through them and threw away dozens of books that contained humanistic and other worldviews that were contrary to the true light of Jesus Christ, the Word of God. Jesus said, *"The lamp of the body is the eye. If therefore your eye is good, your whole body will be full of light. But if your eye is bad, your whole body will be full of darkness. If therefore the light that is in you is darkness, how great is that darkness"* (Matthew 6:22-23)! As believers, we can help the lamps of our bodies (our eyes) by eliminating sources of spiritual darkness from our surroundings when we have the authority to do so. We went through our entire house and trashed anything which might provide an avenue for the entrance of the deceptions of our spiritual enemy, the devil.

We became much more careful regarding what we watched on television. Even then, many of the programs were under the control of that deceiver, the devil. We used the parental controls available on our television set to protect our family and began to use the discernment that comes through the light of Christ in our program selections. Television and the internet are being used both for good and evil. We have a choice as to what we allow into our homes and hearts.

I also did a house cleaning at my office where I worked. I was the boss there and had the authority to do so. This action was a witness to those who worked for me, and some of them eventually surrendered their hearts to Jesus. My actions also generated some harsh words against me. We owned the office building where I worked. I had the cigarette vending machines removed. Immediately, angry smokers lined up to voice their complaints. I told them that I could not be a part of the destruction of their health. This was at a time when a large percentage of the general population smoked, so my decision was not a popular one. When we come to Christ and decide to let His light shine through us, we must remember we are not in a popularity contest but rather one of truth and love. Jesus had delivered me from a chain-smoking tobacco addiction, and I was not going to be a part of enabling others to destroy their health.

John referred to Jesus as *"the Word"* in chapter one of his gospel (John 1:1, 14). One of the main ways to remove dark clouds and open the skies over the gardens of our hearts to the true light of Jesus is to read and meditate daily on the Scriptures, the written Word of God. When we turn on His light, darkness vanishes just as surely it does when one flips on a light switch upon entering a darkened room. As the apostle put it in John 1:5: *"And the light shines in the darkness, and the darkness did not comprehend it."* The phrase *"did not comprehend it"* can be translated to mean "could not constrain it." Darkness cannot constrain the light of God's Word! When God's Word is turned on in our hearts, darkness has to go!

Psalm 119:130 states, *"The entrance of Your words gives light; It gives understanding to the simple."* Sadly, a lot of very smart people have missed the beautiful wisdom of God's Word and sit in spiritual and mental darkness with their intellectualism. Thinking they are wise; they have become fools (Romans 1:22). I know because I used to be one of them. In school I scored very high on mental aptitude tests. I remember scoring highest in the nation on a mathematics test when I was in the ninth grade. I only missed one question. My teacher told me that the national administrators told her that they were very glad that I missed the answer to that one math problem because their policy was that if a student received a perfect score, they were required to generate a completely new test nationwide. I thought I was smart, and I relied on my intellect to work my way up the ladder of success. All the while, that deceiver, the devil, was having a field day with my mistakes. In the wake of my life's path were the tragedies of misdirection, addictions, and pride. I thank God that He brought me to the place of humility, decision, and repentance.

Psalm 119:105 also describes the Word of God as a light: *"Your word is a lamp to my feet and light to my path."* As believers, we need a steady diet of God's Word. The garden of grace that God has set up in our hearts craves the light of His Word daily. When we sit in that beautiful gazebo of grace, that secret meeting place in our hearts, with our Bibles in hand, we often receive direction from the light of God's Word. The Holy Spirit breathes on the Scriptures and brings them to life for us. Sometimes, only the next step is shown to us, and sometimes we are allowed to see further down His pathway for us. Whether it's one step or a whole map, there is comfort in knowing that the plans for our lives are in His hands.

Proverbs 20:27 states, *"The spirit of a man is the lamp of the LORD, searching all the inner depths of his heart."* In

Psalm 18:28, David said, *"For You will light my lamp; The LORD my God will enlighten my darkness."* As we yield ourselves to the Word of God and to the Holy Spirit, He brings to light His plans and purposes for our lives. He also brings to light those things in our hearts that we need to take to the cross in repentance. Sunlight has sanitizing qualities. Many harmful germs thrive in darkness and have difficulty surviving in direct sunlight. The light of the Son of God has spiritual sanitizing properties. The germs of deception and sin cannot survive in His light.

John 1:5-10 describes this cleansing process: *5 This is the message which we have heard from Him and declare to you, that God is light and in Him is no darkness at all. 6 If we say that we have fellowship with Him, and walk in darkness, we lie and do not practice the truth. 7 But if we walk in the light as He is in the light, we have fellowship with one another, and the blood of Jesus Christ His Son cleanses us from all sin. 8 If we say that we have no sin, we deceive ourselves, and the truth is not in us. 9 If we confess our sins, He is faithful and just to forgive us our sins and to cleanse us from all unrighteousness. 10 If we say that we have not sinned, we make Him a liar, and His word is not in us.*

When we were born again, we did not become perfect. We still make mistakes. As we allow the light of His Word and His Spirit to search the depths of our hearts, our sins are revealed. Through confession to God, we can be cleansed from them by the blood of Jesus. God already knows when we miss the mark. We might as well be honest with Him. God is love, and He wants us to be free. He has called us out of darkness into His marvelous light (1 Peter 2:9). His mercy seat is always there in our hearts, waiting for our conversations and visits with Him. As I have said before, we should never run away from God with our sins. We should always run toward Him.

Until we talk it over with Him, we will not be cleansed from the guilt and shame. True freedom and forgiveness only come through Jesus.

Unlike the natural gardens of this world, the garden of grace that Jesus brings to the believer's heart is not stationary. We are mobile, and the gardens of our lives go where we go. One might say that we are gardens with feet. In 1 John 1:7 above, the Bible speaks of our *"walk in the light."* Paul tells us in Ephesians 5:8: *"For you were once darkness, but now are light in the Lord. Walk as children of light."* He wants the light of His Gospel to shine through us to lost and hurting humanity. Jesus called His disciples (including us today) "the light of the world" (Mathew 4:14).

During the shelter in place phase of the Covid-19 crisis, my wife and I looked forward to walks together in our neighborhood. It felt good to get out of the house. The sunlight felt warm and nourishing as it saturated our bodies during our walks. Part of the collateral damage of the shelter in place directives were depression and anxiety. Getting out of the house by walking around the neighborhood was a great antidote for us. According to an article by Rachel Nall entitled *What Are the Benefits of Sunlight*: "Exposure to sunlight is thought to increase the brain's release of a hormone called serotonin. Serotonin is associated with boosting mood and helping a person feel calm and focused."[16]

Just as walking in sunlight can benefit us physically, walking in the light of the Son of God can benefit us spiritually. When we feel discouraged or depressed, we can choose to walk in His light by getting out and encouraging someone else. As we allow His light to shine through us, He increases the light of His presence shining to us. Grace, that divine influence in our hearts, shines brightest when it is reflected through our lives to others! As we get on the move, we become mirrors of Christ's unmerited mercy.

Regarding reaching out to others, Isaiah 58:10-11 states: *10 If you extend your soul to the hungry And satisfy the afflicted soul, Then your light shall dawn in the darkness, And your darkness shall be as the noonday. 11 The Lord will guide you continually, And satisfy your soul in drought, And strengthen your bones; You shall be like a watered garden, And like a spring of water, whose waters do not fail.* A good way to end the drought of depression and discouragement is to get on the move by encouraging and reaching out to others with the light of Jesus. Your walking in His light might be praying for someone, or it might be a charitable act. Sometimes just a warm smile can light another person's countenance. We should remember that we are carriers of gardens of grace.

The following prayer is offered to help in your commitment to grow and walk in His light:

Dear Jesus, You are the light of the world, and You are the light of my life. You are the true light. As I spend time with You in the secret place of the gazebo of grace in my heart, please cause Your light to shine throughout the garden of my life. Show me anything that I need to take to the cross in repentance. Help me to walk in Your light. May Your Word truly be a lamp to my feet and a light to my path. May Your love and grace shine through me to a lost and hurting world. Help me to always remember that I am a carrier of light and not of darkness. May Your grace, like a garden, flourish in my heart and life and become a beacon of hope and truth to others. Amen.

Chapter 9

Plowing with Grace

In most large gardens and farms, plowing is required to break up fallow ground and to prepare rows for the sowing of seeds. In Bible times, plows consisted of metal blades attached to wooden frames and were often pulled by oxen. The farmer's job was to hold the plow in place and keep it steady. In the Bible, we see imageries of grace both in the work of the farmer and of the oxen.

Luke 9:57-62 helps us to understand plowing with grace from the perspective of the farmer: *57 Now it happened as they journeyed on the road, that someone said to Him, "Lord, I will follow You wherever You go." 58 And Jesus said to him, "Foxes have holes and birds of the air have nests, but the Son of Man has nowhere to lay His head." 59 Then He said to another, "Follow Me." But he said, "Lord, let me first go and bury my father." 60 Jesus said to him, "Let the dead bury their own dead, but you go and preach the kingdom of God." 61 And another also said, "Lord, I will follow You, but let me first go and bid them farewell who are at my house." 62 But Jesus said to him, "No one, having put his hand to the plow, and looking back, is fit for the kingdom of God."*

In these verses, Jesus warns against *"looking back."* An experienced farmer knows that he cannot plow a straight row if he is constantly looking back. To plow straight rows, he needs to fix his attention on an immovable object in front of him such as a tree or fence post. Grace and truth come to us through Jesus Christ (John 1:17). In order to plow with grace, the believer should focus his attention on Jesus *"the author and finisher of our faith"* (Hebrews 12:2). This is done through prayer and meditation on the Word of God.

Jesus is the Word. He has always been the Word. He was the Word before the beginning of time. He was the Word during creation. He was the Word throughout the Old Testament. He was the Word when He was born of the Virgin Mary. He was the Word when He was crucified. He was the Word when He was resurrected. He is the Word that is seated at the right hand of God the Father. And He is the Word that is living in our hearts! The Bible, the written Word of God is all about the Word, Jesus.

John 1:1-4,14: *1 In the beginning was the Word, and the Word was with God, and the Word was God. 2 He was in the beginning with God. 3 All things were made through Him, and without Him nothing was made that was made. 4 In Him was life, and the life was the light of men. 14 And the Word became flesh and dwelt among us, and we beheld His glory, the glory as of the only begotten of the Father, full of grace and truth.*

Hebrews 13:8 tells us, *"Jesus Christ is the same yesterday, today, and forever."* Unlike political correctness and the misguided relative moral value systems of today, the moral absolutes of God's Word do not change. Jesus, the Word, is that immovable object at the end of the field that we, as farmers in God's kingdom, should fix our attention on if we are to plow straight rows in the garden of grace.

Jesus identified Himself as *"the bread of life"* in John 6:35. In a recent service at The Lord's Glory Church, my son Brandon gave the following word of exhortation: "In order to enjoy the fresh bread of life that God has for us, we have to let go of the stale bread of the past." This is very true!

Some of the things that can cause us to look back are guilt over past mistakes and sins, trying to relive the past in our minds, procrastination regarding pressures from unbelievers in one's family or community, and traditions that do not agree with the direction of the Holy Spirit for our lives. When Jesus told the man to *"let the dead bury their own dead"* (Luke 9:60), He was not telling him to disregard a funeral service in respect of a deceased family member. The man's request for delay in following Jesus actually involved his staying in his father's employment in order to ensure his obtaining his inheritance. This waiting period could have involved many years. Plowing with grace requires giving top priority to God's calling and plan for one's life. God's grace flows with His lordship. As we have mentioned earlier, *Strong's* defines *charis* (the Greek word for grace) as "the divine influence upon the heart, and its reflection in the life."[17] For that divine influence to be reflected in one's life, one must be willing to obey its direction.

God has already laid out the fields of our lives, and He has given to each of us a spiritual plow which is not directed by the flesh but by grace. The resulting crop of good works in our lives does not earn us God's grace, but rather it is the result of God's grace. Ephesians 2:8-10 helps us to understand the connection between grace and works: *8 For by grace you have been saved through faith, and that not of yourselves; it is the gift of God, 9 not of works, lest anyone should boast. 10 For we are His workmanship, created in Christ Jesus for good works, which God prepared beforehand that we should walk in them.* Our good works do not produce grace, but God's grace does produce good works. It is not works for grace but grace for works. Trying to produce grace by our works is like trying to hitch a plow in front of a team of oxen rather than behind them. It's like trying to pull the oxen with the plow rather than vice versa. We get all worn out, trampled upon, and we don't make any progress.

Once we come to Jesus, we need to put our hands on the plow He has given us and not look back. Instead of trying to review and relive our past mistakes in our minds, we need to leave them at the cross of Christ through repentance. Otherwise, we are not plowing with grace but with condemnation. Paul wrote, *"There is therefore now no condemnation to those who are in Christ Jesus, who do not walk according to the flesh, but according to the Spirit"* (Romans 8:1). When we do not release the guilt and shame of our past mistakes to the cleansing work of the blood of Jesus, we are walking in the flesh. But when we look ahead to Jesus with a clear conscience, we are walking in the Spirit. When our spiritual enemy, the devil, the accuser of the brethren, tries to lay a guilt trip on us over our past, we need to keep plowing the row that God has set before us by saying: "I am a new creation. I am not the person you are talking about. I am not the person I used to be! That person died on the cross with Jesus and was buried with Him. I have been raised in newness of life. The same Spirit that raised Jesus from the dead dwells in me" (see Romans 6:4, 8:11).

Paul said, *"Therefore, if anyone is in Christ, he is a new creation; old things have passed away; behold all things have become new"* (2 Corinthians 5:17). John the Revelator recorded the following: *Then He who sat on the throne said, "Behold I make all things new." And He said to me, "Write, for these words are true and faithful"* (Revelation 21:5). Words of grace come to us from the throne of grace. Plowing with grace recognizes the One Who sits on the throne as Lord and Creator.

He is the One Who makes all things new. Once we put our hands to the plow, we need to fix our attention on Him. This means spending time with Him in His Word and in prayer, and it means closing out the distractions of the past. It means listening for that still, small voice of the Holy Spirit. *"For as many as are led by the Spirit of God, these are sons of God"* (Romans 8:14).

Look at some of those who followed Jesus. They did not let their pasts hold them back. Mary Magdalene had been demon possessed, yet she became a devout disciple of Jesus. Matthew was a despised tax collector, but he became an apostle. According to legend, the woman who was caught in the act of adultery later became the matriarch of the church in Spain. Paul, Saul of Tarsus, was a great enemy of the church. He took part in the persecution, imprisonment, and even execution of both men and women who were early believers in Christ; yet he became possibly the greatest apostle of his time. Once these men and women put their hands to the plow, they did not look back, except to give glory to God and to thank Him for their deliverance. They looked to Jesus and followed Him!

We need to accept the gospel truth that Jesus Christ, our sinless Savior, not only took the judgment and punishment for our sins on the cross at Calvary; He also bore the shame of our sins. I personally believe that this was a very great part of His suffering for us. Hebrews 12:1-2 tells us that He despised the shame but was willing to endure it for the joy that was set before Him. I believe that a major part of that joy was seeing us experience His saving grace: *1 Therefore we also, since we are surrounded by so great a cloud of witnesses, let us lay aside every weight, and the sin which so easily ensnares us, and let us run with endurance the race that is set before us, 2 looking unto Jesus, the author and finisher of our faith, who for the joy that was set before Him endured the cross, despising the shame, and has sat down at the right hand of the throne of God.* Plowing with grace means plowing without the heavy burden of guilt and shame for our past mistakes. Paul said, *"For He made Him who knew no sin to be sin for us, that we might become the righteousness of God in Him"* (2 Corinthians 5:21).

Unforgiveness toward those who have hurt us can also be a major cause of looking back. Putting one's hand to the plow means forgiving those who have hurt or abused us. Forgiving those who have injured us physically or emotionally involves making a decision to stop going over the abuse in our minds. We have to decide to finally put it behind us, put our hand on the plow of grace and focus our attention on Jesus and the future that He has for us. Unforgiveness keeps the plow of grace in the barn rather than in the field where it can work.

We cannot live in the past. Paul said, *"Brethren, I do not count myself to have apprehended; but one thing I do, forgetting those things which are behind and reaching forward to those things which are ahead, I press toward the goal for the prize of the upward call of God in Christ Jesus"* (Philippians 3:13-14). Paul had put his hand to the plow that God had given him. He had decided to continue to direct his attention to Jesus, the One he had encountered on the road to Damascus and the One Who one day would call him home. He had decided not to let anything, including persecutions or successes, stop him from continuing to plow the field that the Lord had set before him. Jesus said, *"And behold, I am coming quickly, and My reward is with Me, to give to every one according to his work"* (Revelation 22:12). Paul refused to be dragged down or distracted by unforgiveness or by the accolades of man. He was determined to plow his field which included much of the most influential portion of the Roman Empire, and his ministry reaches us to-day through his letters in the Bible. He was determined to keep his hand on the plow. He had set his sights on the *"the prize of the upward call"* which most certainly included hearing the words *"well done, good and faithful servant"* (Matthew 25:21). Regardless of the field God has given us, we would all do well to follow the example of Paul.

In the Bible we also see a picture of grace in the work of the oxen who pull the plow. In Matthew 11:28-30, Jesus talked about His yoke: *28 Come to Me, all you who labor and are heavy laden, and I will give you rest. 29 Take My yoke upon you and learn from Me, for I am gentle and lowly in heart, and you will find rest for your souls. 30 For My yoke is easy and My burden is light."* Grace stays step in step with Jesus. He is our lead ox. His yoke is not one of abrasive legalistic works and rituals. His yoke is one of grace.

We are yoked with Jesus through the Holy Spirit. The Holy Spirit descended upon Jesus in the form of a dove when He was baptized by John the Baptist in the Jordan River: *When He had been baptized, Jesus came up immediately from the water; and behold, the heavens were opened to Him, and He saw the Spirit of God descending like a dove and alighting upon Him. And suddenly a voice came from heaven, saying, "This is My beloved Son, in whom I am well pleased"*(Matthew 4:16-17). A dove is a gentle bird and not a bird of prey. Feathers are not heavy; they are light. Here we have a picture of the gentleness of the Holy Spirit.

All of the supernatural works and miracles done by Jesus while here in His human body on the earth were done through the anointing of the Holy Spirit. The same Holy Spirit has been poured out for believers today and yokes us with our Lord and Savior Jesus Christ, the Anointed One. It is the Holy

Spirit that destroys the abrasive yoke of the fleshly, legalistic works of self-righteousness. The Prophet Isaiah connected the anointing oil with the breaking and destruction of the yoke of Assyrian oppression off of the neck and shoulder of Israel: *It shall come to pass in that day that his burden will be taken away from your shoulder, and his yoke from your neck, and the yoke will be destroyed because of the anointing oil* (Isaiah 10:7). The anointing oil represents the Holy Spirit Who sets us free today from all kinds of spiritual and mental oppression. The Holy Spirit teaches us about Jesus. He keeps us in step with our gentle and powerful Christ (The Anointed One).

Going back to Proverbs 3:5-6, our objective should not be to move God but, rather, to move with God*: 5 Trust in the Lord with all your heart, And lean not on your own understanding; 6 In all your ways acknowledge Him, And He shall direct your paths.* The Hebrew word used here for *acknowledge* is *yada.* According to *Strong's, yada* can mean to "be aware" or to "discern."[18] Religious legalism carries the thought that one can buy his way with God, whereas grace carries the thought of flowing with God. Grace means staying in step with our lead ox, the Lord Jesus. To do this, we need to stay within the yoke of the Holy Spirit and resist putting on the yoke of rough, hard religious legalism and fleshly works.

If we will keep our hands on the plow and stay yoked and in step with Jesus, the Anointed One, I believe that we will see God's plans fulfilled for our lives individually and corporately. Furthermore, the church will experience a great end-time harvest like the one prophesied by Amos concerning the regathering of Israel: *"Behold, the days are coming," says the Lord, "When the plowman shall overtake the reaper, And the treader of grapes him who sows seed; The mountains shall drip with sweet wine, And all the hills shall flow with it"* (Amos 9:13).

The following prayer is offered to help you in your commitment to plow with grace:

Dear God, help me to keep my eyes on Your Son Jesus and my hands on the plow of grace. Help me to know when I am looking back rather than ahead to Jesus, the author and finisher of my faith. Help me to repent by turning my attention back to Jesus whenever distractions happen. I commit myself to the yoke of the Holy Spirit that Jesus has given me, and I am determined to resist putting on the yoke of rough, hard religious legalism and fleshly works. May the row that I plow be set by You. I choose not to lean on my own understanding but on acknowledgement of Your providence for my life as revealed to me by the Word and the Spirit. May I be able to say as Paul did, *"Brethren, I do not count myself to have apprehended; but one thing I do, forgetting those things which are behind and reaching forward to those things which are ahead, I press toward the goal for the prize of the upward call of God in Christ Jesus"* (Philippians 3:13-14). My greatest desire is to hear, *"Well done, good and faithful servant"* (Matthew 25:21). In the name of Jesus, amen.

Chapter 10

Pruning in the Garden of Grace

In many of our minds, the word "pruning" brings connotations of pain. I suppose this is because it involves cutting off a branch or stem from a tree or plant. According to garden expert Mike Quinn, "There's no other task that strikes fear into the heart of most amateur gardeners as does the subject of pruning plants. Yet successful pruning can be among the most satisfying of garden tasks, because the results can be spectacular. Pruning done correctly yields abundant flowers, foliage and fruit. Pruning done incorrectly results in damaged plants, disappointment and failure! No wonder we fear the process."[19]

Pruning in the gardens of our lives is the work of our Heavenly Father Who loves us. It is part of His grace. He knows what we need for good, productive growth, and He knows what we don't need. He knows what's good for us, and He knows what's bad for us.

Jesus described the spiritual pruning process in John 15:1-8: *1 "I am the true vine, and My Father is the vinedresser. 2 Every branch in Me that does not bear fruit He takes away; and every branch that bears fruit He prunes, that it may bear more fruit. 3 You are already clean because of the word which I have spoken to you. 4 Abide in Me, and I in you. As the branch cannot bear fruit of itself, unless it abides in the vine, neither can you, unless you abide in Me. 5 I am the vine, you are the branches. He who abides in Me, and I in him, bears much fruit; for without Me you can do nothing. 6 If anyone does not abide in Me, he is cast out as a branch and is withered; and they gather them and throw them into the fire, and they are burned. 7 If you abide in Me, and My words abide in you, you will ask what you desire, and it shall be done for you. 8 By this My Father is glorified, that you bear much fruit; so you will be My disciples."*

From these verses, it is clear that Jesus is the true vine (v.1). Any branch that does not abide in Him is not part of the true vine and is headed for a withered life and a final destination of eternal fire (v.6). These tragic branches would include those who say they are Christians but have not truly surrendered their hearts to Jesus. Those of us who have sincerely and truly accepted Jesus and found our lives in Him are branches of the true vine (v.5). We are pruned by God the Father, the vine-dresser, so that we may bear more fruit (v.2). This pruning process involves God clipping off twigs and stems in our lives which are contrary to His plan for us. In this way the twigs and stems which have fruit bearing potential are not drained of nourishment by non-fruit bearing growth and can more fully develop as fruit bearers themselves.

Abiding in the Word of God is a key to bearing much fruit as disciples of Christ (vv.7-8). The Word is one of the titles of Jesus (John 1:1,14). In John 6:63, Jesus said, *"The words that I speak to you are spirit, and they are life."* As we read and meditate daily on the Scriptures, the vines of our lives are being nourished and strengthened in Christ, so that we can bear much fruit.

Our fruit should certainly include the fruit of the Spirit which is *"love, joy, peace, longsuffering, kindness, goodness, faithfulness, gentleness, self-control"* (Galatians 5:22-23).

When we inspect the fruit of our lives, it should all be flavored with love. We will find upon close inspection, that the stems of our vines pruned by the Father's providence include those that were not conceived in love. As we continue to read in John 15, we will see that Jesus confirms the connection between abiding in His love and bearing much fruit.

John 15:9-17: *9 "As the Father loved Me, I also have loved you; abide in My love. 10 If you keep My commandments, you will abide in My love, just as I have kept My Father's commandments and abide in His love. 11 These things I have spoken to you, that My joy may remain in you, and that your joy may be full. 12 This is My commandment, that you love one another as I have loved you.13 Greater love has no one than this, than to lay down one's life for his friends. 14 You are My friends if you do whatever I command you. 15 No longer do I call you servants, for a servant does not know what his master is doing; but I have called you friends, for all things that I heard from My Father I have made known to you. 16 You did not choose Me, but I chose you and appointed you that you should go and bear fruit, and that your fruit should remain, that whatever you ask the Father in My name He may give you. 17 These things I command you, that you love one another.*

To me, love is like that juice or sap that drips from a plant or tree when a stem or limb is cut off. It is the life of the plant. Many of the stems and limbs that God prunes are the dry, dead ones that are void of real love. They are just taking up space. When we choose love for direction at the crossroads of decisions, we are likely to experience less dead, dry growth developing in our lives. For example, it is easy to fall into the trap of being led by opportunity rather than by love and the Holy Spirit. If the enemy knows we are being led by opportunity, he will bring more opportunity than we can handle in order to drain our strength. God's grace operates beautifully in our lives and ministries when we choose those good works *"which God pre-pared beforehand that we should walk in them"* (Ephesians 2:10b).

As we walk through the Gospel with Jesus, we often read that He was moved with compassion before doing miracles. For example in the very first chapter of Mark, we read that Jesus was moved with compassion before healing a leper who came to Him (Mark 1:41). On a trip to Israel, I learned that there had been a large leper colony in the region where Jesus did many of His miracles, yet there is no record of His having gone to that colony to heal them. In Mark 8:2, Jesus said *"I have compassion on the multitude, because they have now continued with Me three days and have nothing to eat."* After making this statement, Jesus fed four thousand families with seven loaves of bread and a few fish which He miraculously multiplied. There were certainly many other hungry people in Israel during that time of Roman tyranny and taxation who were not miraculously fed. Jesus was moved by compassion. We should be moved by compassion. Having said this, Jesus did go to the cross so that all who come to Him can believe and have hope in the New Covenant promises, including healing and provision. Jesus kept the divine appointments for His ministry, including going to the cross, by being moved with compassion rather than opportunity or need, and so should we.

Before undertaking a project to meet a need, we should search our hearts for compassion. If the compassion is not there, or if that gentle nudge or prompting of the Holy Spirit is not there, we should reassess our potential involvement. Many of the stems and branches of our lives and ministries that are eventually pruned by the Father are those dry ones that were not motivated by love. We can not meet every need we see, but we can have confidence that we can meet those appointed to us by God.

God's ways are not the ways of man, and we should seek His way of providing help to others. On my first ministry trip to India in 1988, I was overwhelmed by the poverty I saw in Bombay (now Mumbai). At that time, Bombay had the largest number of homeless people of any city in the world. I literally saw adults and children starving to death on the streets. Following is an article I wrote for Mahaneh Dan Fellowship's Silver Jubilee Anniversary Magazine. It describes the way the Holy Spirit moved on my heart to help the people of India.

Congratulations to Mahaneh- Dan Fellowship on this 25th year Silver Jubilee anniversary. It has indeed been an honor to be associated with this wonderful ministry all of these years. Some of my fondest memories of ministry have been experiences that my family and I have had in India working with Pastor P. T. Varghese and the many other dedicated brothers and sisters in Christ, which make up the ever-growing Mahaneh-Dan Fellowship. Your faith, courage, humility, and love have always been an inspiration to us.

India has a special place in our hearts. I love India. I love the way it feels. I love the way it smells. I love the colorful clothes, the varieties of foods, the different cultures within the country itself, and the way everything is always moving. The modes of transportation are unequaled in variety ...... motor bikes, rickshaws, auto rickshaws, cars, vans, taxi cabs, trucks of all kinds, elephants, oxcarts, bicycles, trains, airplanes, foot, and I'm sure I have left some out. My wife, my son, and I have traveled to many countries, and we can say that India is the most interesting place on earth to us. The people of India are really amazing! They are full of enthusiasm and energy. They always seem to be on the go, and there are so many of them! I believe the only time in India that I remember not seeing people everywhere was my last trip in 2011 when my son and I traveled by van through a national park. Yes, I love India. Most of all, I love its people.

My first trip to India was from late December 1987 to mid-January 1988. At that time Mumbai had the largest number of homeless people of any city in the world. Riding through one area of the city, I saw countless numbers of people, including children, living under pieces of cardboard or whatever material they could find to lean against walls for shelter. Many of the children were without clothing, and there was obviously a shortage of food. From the back of an auto rickshaw, the needs I saw were overwhelming. I left a very successful career in the oil industry when God called me into ministry. I remember thinking, "If I had all the money I had ever made in the oil industry, I could give it away from the back of this rickshaw and not even make a noticeable difference."

In my frustration, I recalled a story I had read about a man named Ludwig who had devised a plan many years ago to help impoverished people living along the Amazon River in South America. Ludwig, who in his day was considered the wealthiest man in the United States, had two huge pulpwood plants floated over to South America from Japan and set up on an area of the Amazon. The trees in the area were enormous and well suited for the manufacture of paper. Ludwig hired thousands of the local people and paid them very well to work harvesting the trees and running the mills. While his motives for this project were very noble, the results were disastrous. Houses of prostitution, gambling casinos, bars, and drug dealers set up directly across the river from Ludwig's plants. The results were venereal disease, alcoholism, drug addiction, destroyed families, and worse poverty than ever before. Not only that, Ludwig had failed to do an accurate ecological study of the area. The large trees he harvested had taken many centuries to grow, and the soil was not suitable for replanting with fast growing trees. The land was ruined, and Ludwig lost most of his fortune.

One man with a Bible could have helped the people more than all of Ludwig's millions, because true prosperity begins with a change of heart. I determined that day as these thoughts went through my mind that the best way to help the people of India was to help in the spreading of the Gospel of Jesus Christ. Jesus came that we might have life and have it more abundantly (John 10:10).

On that very first trip to India, I also met Pastor P.T. Varghese and was very impressed with his integrity, humility, and total dedication to the Lord Jesus Christ and the Word of God. My family and I (and later The Lord's Glory Church) have been sowing our prayers, financial support, and ministry trips into Mahaneh-Dan Fellowship from its inception and have been overjoyed to see its spreading the Gospel all over India with hundreds of church plantings, Bible and ministry training schools, a Christian high school, jobs skills schools, and orphanages. These efforts are bringing real help and blessing to the people of India, and we thank God that we have had the opportunity to be a partner with Pastor Varghese and all the other precious members of Mahaneh-Dan Fellowship. May your greatest days be ahead! [20]

All believers experience times when they think they are hearing from God regarding a project, yet pruning takes place anyway. Mature believers recognize they can miss God with their decisions and are willing to accept His pruning of well-intentioned endeavors. Often, the person is hearing from God regarding a ministry or work but is going about it in a way that does not fit God's plans. In other words, they have the right dream but the wrong blueprint. They have the correct destination but are following the wrong map. In this type of pruning we need to be careful not to get discouraged or bitter.

Instead, we should continue to trust in God, knowing that His providence is working in our lives for what is good according to Romans 8:28: *And we know that all things work together for good to those who love God, to those who are the called according His purpose.*

My son, Brandon, had it in his heart to work with orphans after he graduated from Christ for the Nations Institute (CFNI) in Dallas, Texas. He applied to work with a ministry in Mexico that helped orphans. He never heard back from them. It was as though God had pruned that stem from the vine of his ministry. Meanwhile a youth pastor position opened for him with a church in Kingwood, Texas. After a successful year with that church, he perceived in his heart that his time there was coming to a close. He told the pastor that he felt like God had something else for him. Little did he know that on the same day he met with his pastor, the Lord moved on his parents' hearts to plant The Lord's Glory Church. We were ministering in Argentina at the time and had not discussed our decision with him prior to making it. After hearing of it, Brandon realized that the Lord was calling him to help pioneer this new church. We started the church in January of 1995. In December of 1996, Brandon married Sarah who had been a classmate of his at CFNI. All this time the dream to work with orphans was still in Brandon's heart and also in Sarah's.

It has now been over a quarter of a century since the founding of The Lord's Glory Church. Brandon and Sarah have adopted two beautiful children, a daughter from China and a son from Ethiopia. They are also advocates for orphans and international adoption. They have worked closely with America World Adoption in speaking at seminars and advising prospective adoptive parents. We and others have caught the dream with them. Our church helps support orphanages in several different countries. Brandon had the right dream all along, but

God had His way of it being fulfilled. While pruning in the garden of our lives can sometimes seem painful, we need to recognize that God's grace is always at work. Truly all things have worked together for good for my son and his wife, as their dream of working with orphans is being fulfilled in the most wonderful way, including parenting. I marvel as I think of how God has placed a jewel from China and a jewel from Ethiopia in our family's crown!

As we can see from Brandon's experience, God's pruning of a stem does not necessarily mean the cutting off of a dream. Look at the life of Joseph in the Old Testament. When he was seventeen, he had a dream that one day he would be the patriarch of his family. He made the mistake of sharing his dream with his older brothers, who were already jealous of him because of his favorite son status with Jacob, their father. Nothing seemed to work out for Joseph concerning his dream. After nearly killing him, his brothers sold him to slave traders. They, in turn, sold him to Potiphar, who was the captain of the guard and the chief executioner of Egypt. Potiphar recognized Joseph's leadership skills, and he put him in charge of all his household and business affairs. But Potiphar's wife made sexual advances toward Joseph. After Joseph resisted her, she falsely accused him of trying to molest her. Remarkably, instead of being executed, Joseph was imprisoned.

No matter the circumstances in which Joseph found himself, the patriarchal anointing of leadership necessary for the carrying out of his dream remained upon him. Just as Potiphar had placed Joseph over his business affairs, the keeper of the prison soon recognized Joseph's wisdom and leadership skills and put him in charge of all the other prisoners.

When Joseph received his dream of becoming his family's patriarch, he also obviously received the gift of interpreting dreams. Two high-profile prisoners, the chief butler and the chief baker of the king of Egypt, had offended their master and were in prison with Joseph. They both had disturbing dreams and came to Joseph for interpretation. Joseph correctly interpreted their dreams. According to Joseph's interpretations, within three days, the chief butler would be restored to his previous position with Pharaoh, and the chief baker would be executed. Everything happened as Joseph had said. Joseph asked the chief butler to petition Pharaoh for his release, but the chief butler soon forgot Joseph.

After two full years, Pharaoh had dreams that none of his wise men could interpret. The chief butler at that time remembered Joseph and mentioned him to his master. Immediately, Pharaoh called for Joseph who correctly interpreted his dreams to mean seven years of abundant harvest for Egypt followed by seven years of extreme famine. Furthermore, Joseph advised Pharaoh to store grain during the good years so that the nation would not perish during the years of famine. Pharaoh was so impressed that he placed Joseph in charge of Egypt's economy. As it turned out, all the nations around Egypt also experienced the seven years of famine and came to Joseph in Egypt to buy grain. Think about this. In one day's time, Joseph went from being a prisoner to being placed in charge of the world's economy!

Among those traveling to Egypt to buy grain were Joseph's brothers. The same brothers who sold Joseph into slavery were now at his mercy, although they did not recognize Joseph until he eventually revealed himself to them. As it turned out, Joseph's entire family was saved from the worldwide famine through him. Joseph could have let a root of bitterness take hold of him as God's providential pruning took place in his life with accompanying trials and tests. Instead, he continued to trust in God, and the results were the preserving, strengthening, and positioning of the patriarchal trunk of his life and his dream. His brothers were afraid that he would avenge their harsh treatment of him, but he reassured them of his forgiveness with these words in Genesis 50:20-21: *"But as for you, you meant evil against me; but God meant it for good, in order to bring about as it is this day, to save many people alive. Now therefore, do not be afraid; I will provide for you and your little ones." And he comforted them and spoke kindly to them.*

The nations were saved from starving during the worldwide famine, and the family of Israel, through whom the Messiah eventually came to humanity, was preserved because this man Joseph refused to look on God's pruning as tragedy. Instead, his life, his dream, and his gift matured and bore the fruit of God's prophetic plans. Joseph looked for and found grace every step of the way. He never gave up on his dream or his gift. Romans 11:29 states, *"For the gifts and the calling of God are irrevocable."* God may prune opportunities, options, and plans, but He does not prune His grace which includes His gifts and calling.

The following prayer is offered to help you trust in God during seasons of pruning:

Father God, I know that my life is in Your hands and that You have a good plan for me and my ministry. I trust You completely. I am determined to nourish my inner man with Your Word and to be moved by compassion rather than opportunity or need. Help me to be sensitive to the nudges and promptings of Your Spirit. When pruning is necessary in the garden of my life, I will hold on to the gifts and dreams that You have given me, knowing that You are bringing them to fruition in ways that I may not currently understand. Thank You for Your love and Your grace. In the name of Jesus, amen.

118

Chapter 11

Grace for all Seasons

A ll of us experience many seasons in our lives. King Solomon listed some of the seasons he had observed in Ecclesiastes 3:1-8:

1 To everything there is a season, A time for every purpose under heaven: 2 A time to be born, And a time to die; A time to plant, And a time to pluck what is planted; 3 A time to kill, And a time to heal; A time to break down, And a time to build up; 4 A time to weep, And a time to laugh; A time to mourn, And a time to dance; 5 A time to cast away stones, And a time to gather stones; A time to embrace, And a time to refrain from embracing; 6 A time to gain, And a time to lose; A time to keep, And a time to throw away; 7 A time to tear, And a time to sew; A time to keep silence, And a time to speak; 8 A time to love, And a time to hate; A time of war, And a time of peace.

The important thing for the believer to know is that God's grace is there for him or her in every season of life. We are not alone. I started this book writing about a young boy in the 1950s and his garden. As I look back on the garden of my life, I realize that God's grace has been with me in every season of my life. Even when I did not know Him, Jesus was there drawing me to Himself. Seasons come and go, but *"Jesus Christ is the same yesterday, today, and forever"* (Hebrews 13:8).

Paul, who went from being a great persecutor and enemy of the church to becoming a great apostle, summarized his identity and ministry in 1 Corinthians 15:9-10: *For I am the least of the apostles, who am not worthy to be called an apostle, because I persecuted the church of God. But by the grace of God I am what I am, and His grace toward me was not in vain; but I labored more abundantly than they all, yet not I, but the grace of God which was with me.* If we will only release ourselves to His grace in every season of our lives, we will be able to say, as Paul did, "by the grace of God we are what we are." When we try to labor on our own, we accomplish little and only wear out ourselves and those around us.

God's plan for Paul from birth had been to preach the Gospel of Jesus Christ, especially among the Gentiles. God had set Paul apart from birth for this ministry, but his zeal for God actually manifested in his persecuting the church until he had his encounter with Jesus on the road to Damascus. But once he surrendered to Jesus, the same zeal that had previously been misdirected was refocused on reaching the world with the Good News of his Savior and Lord Jesus Christ. Paul describes this redirection of zeal in Galatians 1:13-16: *For you have heard of my former conduct in Judaism, how I persecuted the church of God beyond measure and tried to destroy it. And I advanced in Judaism beyond my contemporaries in my own nation, being more exceedingly zealous for the traditions of my fathers. But when it pleased God, who separated me from my mother's womb and called me through His grace, to reveal His Son in me, that I might preach Him among the Gentiles, I did not immediately confer with flesh and blood.* Paul's zeal was a gift from God from birth, but it was misdirected until he opened his heart to Jesus.

God does not waste anything. His grace will preserve good roots from previous seasons and replant them to use in future seasons. For example, God pulled me out of the business world when I was born again. He immediately placed me in ministry, but the business skills that I learned during my season as a businessman have not been wasted. I have seen many ministries fail because of a lack of basic business acumen. All ministries go through seasons regarding cash flow and expenses. Budgets have to be adjusted accordingly. The Bible, especially the Book of Proverbs, is full of good, sound business advice for individuals, families, businesses, churches, and ministries. God's grace includes impartation of sound wisdom and direction by His Spirit and by His Word regarding financial matters. Also, it is wonderful to know that when our best plans fail, His grace does not fail and is there to lift us up!

I was somewhat well-known as a businessman in my area when I got saved. Many of those who knew me, or knew of me, were astonished when they heard of my salvation. The phone began to ring with invitations from churches and other organizations including Full Gospel Businessmen International to share my testimony. God has used me to minister to many businesspeople over the years.

For the next ten years, my wife and I traveled to many states and countries ministering fulltime as evangelists and teachers. Our season of evangelism gave way to a pastoral ministry in early 1995 when we and our son founded The Lord's Glory Church. As pastors we have also kept a flavor for evangelism in our ministry. Again, there is that carryover of grace from one season to another. Our church supports ministries in other countries, including Mexico, India, Peru, Honduras, Haiti, Uganda, and Israel, to name some. We still occasionally make ministry trips to other countries. This has been healthy for our church. Churches need a world vision. Jesus said, *"Go into all the world and preach the gospel to every creature"* (Mark 16:15). Having a heart for missions keeps churches from becoming little "bless me clubs" and opens the way for rivers of grace.

When I was in high school, the teacher of one my classes had all of her students try their hands at writing a poem. I jotted one down and turned it in. I don't remember much about it, but the teacher and my classmates thought it was really good. It wound up being printed on the front page of the school newsletter. There was a grace for writing even in my teenage years, but it stayed pretty much dormant until after I started serving the Lord. When we come to Jesus, He replants those roots of grace from our old life into the fresh soil of the new birth, where they can bring forth the harvest He intended all along. By His grace, over the years as a believer, I have written more than a few Christ-centered poems, song lyrics, and books. To God be all the glory!

When I was a very young man in the business world, I joined the Junior Chamber of Commerce. One of the Jaycees' projects at that time was a speaking contest. I was asked to enter and won first place in my chapter's competition. I also won first place in the district competition. I was amazed because I did not spend much preparation time. There was a grace for public speaking in my life before coming to Jesus that was replanted in the soil of my new life as a preacher of the Gospel. In the thirty-six years since I answered the call of God, I have preached thousands of messages across the United States and in many other countries as well.

Before making those speeches in the Junior Chamber of Commerce competitions, I relieved my nervousness by drinking alcohol. I thank God that He delivered me from alcoholism when I surrendered to Him. Alcohol and substance abuse are just counterfeits offered by the devil. The body of my flesh, the weakness of my humanity, was looking for liquid courage, something to numb the nerves. What I really needed was the New Wine of the Holy Spirit! His anointing is so much better than alcohol! There's no hangover, and there are no regrets! It's important as believers to leave the counterfeit graces of the enemy behind and to embrace the real graces available to us through the Holy Spirit!

God's grace is there for every season of life and ministry, if we will only look for it. *For He Himself has said, "I will never leave you nor forsake you"* (Hebrews 13:5b). Paul made a plea to all of us in 2 Corinthians 6:1-2: *1 We then, as workers together with Him also plead with you not to receive the grace of God in vain. 2 For He says: "In an acceptable time I have heard you, And in the day of salvation I have helped you." Behold, now is the accepted time; behold, now is the day of salvation.*

The Greek word for *"time"* in verse 2 is *"kairos."* According to Strong's, one of the definitions of *"kairos"* is *"season."*[21] This is another confirmation that God's grace is always with us in every season. We are never alone. *"Salvation"* (Greek *"sotayreeah"*) in verse 2 includes *"rescue"* in Strong's definition.[22] Not only are we saved spiritually by His grace, His grace is there in every season to rescue and deliver us. God's grace is always there for us because Jesus is always with us. Wherever we find ourselves, we need to look to Jesus and pray for His grace. We need to look for His unmerited mercy and favor. We need to act on His divine influence in our hearts. Trying to operate without His grace is like trying to force a square block into a round hole: it just doesn't work. But when we allow His grace to labor through us, as Paul did, things start fitting together.

Obviously we all go through the seasons of childhood, youth, young adult, adult, middle-age, and senior years. Each age level has its challenges. There's grace for parenting, and there's another grace for grandparenting. My wife and I are in the grandparenting stage, and it's a lot of fun. The experience we have had as parents is repackaged by His grace for a less pressured season of grandparenting.

The key is to flow with the Spirit of God in each season of life. Otherwise, we find ourselves trying to swim upstream, which can be difficult and trying. Transition from one age to another can bring crisis unless one leans on the grace of God, seeking His help. If we are not careful, we can find ourselves living in regret, as we try to relive the past, rather than enjoying where we are while we're going where we're going. We need to keep our eyes on Jesus and look for His grace in every season of life. He is always there. As Gordon Jensen's song says, "He's as close as the mention of His name."[23]

Most of us go through seasons of tribulation and testing. We don't ask for them. They just show up. These difficult times can involve persecutions because of our faith in Christ. If we will lean on Jesus, His grace will always be there to get us through. In 2 Corinthians 11, Paul discussed some of the persecutions, distresses, sufferings, and tribulations he had been through for the sake of the Gospel. These included being beaten five times with 39 stripes, another three times with rods, being stoned, being shipwrecked three times, spending a whole day and night in the sea, being in danger from persecutions from his own countrymen and from the Gentiles, experiencing hunger, thirst, a lack of adequate clothing against adverse weather conditions, going without sleep, and other perils, including infirmities.

Paul did not blame God for these trials. He recognized that he had a spiritual enemy, *"a messenger of Satan"* that he referred to as *"a thorn in the flesh"* (2 Corinthians 12:7). In answer to Paul's plea for relief, the Lord said, *"My grace is sufficient for you, for my strength is made perfect in weakness"* (2 Corinthians 12:9). When we find ourselves in challenging seasons of trials and tribulations, we must be careful, like Paul, not to look on God as our enemy. Identifying the enemy is a key to victory. The Lord is on our side and not against us. It is His grace that gets us through. When we turn to the Lord for help, our weakness becomes a magnet for His strength.

Paul understood humanity's vulnerability to pride, which can hinder the believer's access to grace, and he was concerned that the abundance of revelations given to him could cause him to be exalted above measure by his followers (2 Corinthians 12:7). He knew that the humility he was experiencing as a result of these trials only served to place him in position for God's power to work on his behalf. God gives grace to the humble (James 4:6, 1 Peter 5:5). Paul knew that the more he relied on the power of Christ and the less he relied on his own strength, the greater his deliverance and the greater his witness for Jesus. When we understand grace, we can say as Paul did, *"For when I am weak, then I am strong"* (2 Corinthians 12:10). As Isaiah said, *"He gives power to the weak, and to those who have no might He increases strength"* (Isaiah 40:29).

No doubt, Paul was the man who was *"caught up into Paradise and heard inexpressible words which it is not lawful for a man to utter"* (2 Corinthians 12:4). Paul returned from heaven's Paradise with an abundance of revelations that he was allowed to share with us. Much of our understanding of grace comes from the writings of Paul. I believe that most of his revelations of grace were given to him during his time in Paradise, the garden in heaven. Grace truly is like a garden!

The following prayer is offered to help you in your search for God's grace in every season of life:

Dear God, I know that Your grace is always there for me. I am never alone. You are always with me. Help me to recognize the season in which I am living. Please let me know when I am trying to swim upstream against Your plan for me. Help me to flow with Your Spirit. Help me to catch the current of Your grace in every season of life and ministry. May my weaknesses only serve to usher in Your grace, with all its power, for victory against every challenge of the enemy. To You be all the glory forever and ever! In the name of Jesus, amen.

Endnotes

1   Tom Battle, *Paradise*, United States Copyright Office Registration Number Pau3-063-245, 2006

2   *Webster's Seventh New Collegiate Dictionary*, (Springfield, Massachusetts, G. & C. Merriam Company, 1965), 362.

3   James Strong, *The New Strong's Exhaustive Concordance of the Bible with Dictionary of the Greek Testament*, (Nashville, Tennessee, Thomas Nelson Publishers, 1984), 77.

4   Roy B. Zuck, *The Speaker's Quote Book: Over 5,000 Illustrations and Quotations for All Occasions* (Kregel Academic & Professional: Revised and Expanded Edition 2009), //ministry127.com/resources/illustration/children-must-be-taught-while-they-are-young.

5   Strong, *The New Strong's*, 47

6   Ibid., 64

7   Brandon Battle & Real Love. *I Can Count on You*. The Lord's Glory Church, 2007. CD (track 7).

8   "WHEAT," The University of Arizona Cooperative Extension, Agriculture in the Classroom USDA, www.agintheclassroom.org/http://cals.arizona.edu/agliteracy.

9   Sam Martin, *How I Led One and One Led a Million* (United States of America: Martin, 2001).

10 Strong, *The New Strong's,* 77

11 Tom Battle*, Over the Sea,* United States Copyright Office Registration Number Pau2-962-873, 2005.

12 Monique Allen, "The Importance of Water for Your Garden," The Garden Continuum, //www.the gardencontinuum. com, (July 18, 2019).

13 Tom Battle, *Hot Line From God,* (Houston, Battle Ministries, 1989).

14 Charles Spurgeon, "Tears of Those too Weary to Pray," www.pinterest.com.

15 Ivory Harlow, "Sunlight requirements for growing vegetables,"//www.farmanddairy.com, (April 10, 2015).

16 Rachel Nall, RN, BSN, CCRN, "What Are the Benefts of Sunlight," //www.healthline.com/health/depression/benefits-sunlight (updated April 1, 2019).

17 Strong, *The New Strong's,* 77

18 Ibid., 47

19 Mike Quinn, "The Basics of Pruning," //www.gardeners-path.com, (August 15, 2014).

20 Tom Battle, *Silver Jubilee Special Edition Souvenir,* (Mumbai, India, Mahaneh-Dan Fellowship, 2016), 17-18.

21 Strong, *The New Strong's,* 39

22 Ibid., 70

23 Gordon Jenson. *He's as Close as the Mention of His Name.* Gordon Jenson International Ministries, P.O. Box 145, Gallatin, Tennessee 37066, www.gordonjenson.homestead.com.

Appendix A

Scriptures Used in *Grace Like a Garden*

Listed by Chapter

Chapter 1 – Answering His Call

Genesis 3:9	2 Corinthians 5:21
Romans 3:23	John 19:30
2 Peter 3:9	Luke 23:43
Acts 4:12	John 19:41-42
John 14:6	John 20:11-16
1 Peter 2:22-24	

Chapter 2 – Grace for Grace

John 1:16	2 Corinthians 5:17
John 1:1-3	2 Corinthians 5:18-19
John 1:14	Proverbs 11:30
Galatians 3:19	Matthew 10:27
Genesis 3:15	Matthew 5:14-16
Numbers 24:7	Ephesians 2:8-10
Isaiah 53:10	Proverbs 3:5-6
Galatians 3:16	2 Corinthians 3:3
1 Peter 2:23	Galatians 5:22-23
Romans 8:29	1 Corinthians 13:4-8a
John 3:30	John 1:16

Chapter 3 – The Throne of Grace

Galatians 5:19-21	Romans 8:17
Galatians 6:7-8	Hebrews 4:15-16
John 3:36a	John 15:13
John 5:24	1 John 1:9
Hebrews 4:16	Isaiah 1:18
Luke 17:21	Romans 5:17

Romans 5:20-21
John 8:36
John 8:31b-32
John 6:63b
2 Corinthians 3:17
Galatians 5:22-23
Romans 10:17
Romans 5:1-2
Isaiah 55:10-13
Ephesians 3:14-21

Galatians 5:6
Psalm 51:17
Psalm 27:5-9
Psalm 61:4
Acts 15:13-17
John 14:6
1 John 2:2
Exodus 25:17
1 John 4:10
Hebrews 4:16

Chapter 4 – The Power of Seeds

Matthew 17:20
Romans 5:2
Zechariah 4:6-7
Mark 11:22-26
Proverbs 18:21
Deuteronomy 30:19
Psalm 103:1-3
Isaiah 53:5
1 Peter 2:24
Romans 10:17
John 3:16
Romans 10:9-10, 13
1 John 4:18a
2 Timothy 1:7

Philippians 4:6-7
Isaiah 26:3
Romans 14:17
Nehemiah 8:10b
Psalm 118:24
Psalm 30:5b
Philippians 4:4
Matthew 13:3-9
Matthew 13:18-23
Revelation 3:20
Jeremiah 31:34
Matthew 6:24
1 Timothy 6:10

Chapter 5 – The Mathematics of Grace

Matthew 13
Luke 6:38
Galatians 3:16
John 12:23-24
Matthew 9:37-38

Matthew 28:18-20
2 Corinthians 3:3
John 9:9
2 Corinthians 6:1-2

Chapter 6 – Grace in Giving

2 Corinthians 8:1-7
John 3:16
John 19:25
2 Corinthians 9:6-15
Matthew 28:18-20
Genesis 14:20
Genesis 28:22
Hebrews 7:12-14
Hebrews 7:15-17
Hebrews 7:1-3
Galatians 3:5-9
Hebrews 7:8

Hebrews 8:1-2
Matthew 11:10
Malachi 3:10-12
1 Corinthians 15:20
Proverbs 19:17
Proverbs 25:21-22
Matthew 5:43-48
Galatians 6:6-10
Psalm 69:12
1 Chronicles 16:29b
Galatians 6:7
Galatians 6:9

Chapter 7 – Watering Your Garden

Genesis 2:10
John 7:37-39
Titus 3:4-7
Isaiah 55:1
1 Peter 2:2-3
Ephesians 5:18
Acts 1:4-5
John 20:22
Acts 2:1-13
Acts 2:32-33
Acts 2:41
Acts 10:44-47
Acts 19:1-7
Acts 19:10
1 Corinthians 12:10

1 Corinthians 14:39-40
1 Corinthians 14:14a
Jude 20-21
1 Corinthians 14:14-15
Mark 16:17
Luke 11:11-13
Ephesians 5:25-29
Psalm 1:2-3
Psalm 56:8-9
Romans 8:26-27
John 11:32-44
Hebrews 5:7
Ephesians 3:20
Psalm 126:5-6
Psalm 65:9-10

Chapter 8 – Son Light for Your Garden

Genesis 1:3
John 1:1-9
John 8:12
2 Corinthians 11:14
Ephesians 2:1-3
Isaiah 9:1-2
Matthew 4:15-16
John 8:44
Matthew 6:22-23
John 1:1
John 1:14
John 1:5

Psalm 119:130
Romans 1:22
Psalm 119:105
Proverbs 20:27
Psalm 18:28
John 1:5-10
1 Peter 2:9
1 John 1:7
Ephesians 5:8
Matthew 4:14
Isaiah 58:10-11

Chapter 9 – Plowing with Grace

Luke 9:57-62
John 1:17
Hebrews 12:2
John 1:1-4
John 1:14
Hebrews 13:8
John 6:35
Luke 9:60
Ephesians 2:8-10
Romans 8:1
Romans 6:4
Romans 8:11
Revelation 21:5

Romans 8:14
Hebrews 12:1-2
2 Corinthians 5:21
Philippians 3:13-14
Revelation 22:12
Matthew 11:28-30
Matthew 4:16-17
Isaiah 10:7
Proverbs 3:5-6
Amos 9:13
Matthew 25:21

Chapter 10 – Pruning in the Garden of Grace

John 15:1-8

John 1:1, 14

John 6:63

Galatians 5:22-23

John 15:9-17

Ephesians 2:10b

Mark 1:41

Mark 8:2

John 10:10

Romans 8:28

Genesis 50:20-21

Romans 11:29

Chapter 11 – Grace for all Seasons

Ecclesiastes 3:1-8

Hebrews 13:8

1 Corinthians 15:9-10

Galatians 1:13-16

Mark 16:15

Hebrews 13:5b

2 Corinthians 6:1-2

2 Corinthians 11:23-29

2 Corinthians 12:7

2 Corinthians 12:9

James 4:6

1 Peter 5:5

2 Corinthians 12:10

Isaiah 40:29

2 Corinthians 12:4

Appendix B

Salvation Prayer

Lord Jesus, I repent for the way I have been living by turning to You with my whole heart for forgiveness, salvation, and a new beginning. I accept You now and forever as my personal Lord and Savior. Thank You for bringing paradise to my heart and becoming the gardener of my life. In Your name, the name of Jesus, amen.

Author's Credentials

Tom Battle is a graduate of Georgia Tech (1969) and Lakewood Bible Institute (1988). During his business career, he held prominent positions with several oil companies. He reached executive levels of President and CEO before leaving the business world to enter full-time ministry. He was ordained in 1990 by Lakewood Church (Houston, Texas) which was his home church from 1985 to 1995. During that time, he was mentored by Dr. John Osteen and traveled extensively in the United States and abroad as an evangelist and teacher. In 1995 he and his family founded The Lord's Glory Church where he is currently the Senior Pastor. He is the author of many Christian books and songs.

Books by Tom Battle

Face the Solution
Hot Line from God
Love Power
The Heartbeat of God
Touching Jesus
The Healing Leaf
Love is the Greatest
There is Hope
Grace Like a Garden

About the Publisher:

Battle Ministries is a 501(c)3 non-profit corporation founded in 1990 by Tom and Schar Battle. In addition to publishing books written by Tom Battle, it supports charitable and evangelistic Christian works worldwide. Speaking and ministry engagements outside Tom's home church are also arranged by Battle Ministries.

Address: 461 Artesian Plaza Drive
           Humble, Texas 77338-3925
Phone: (281)-446-0091

Visit our online bookstore: www.battleministries.com

Visit Us at The Lord's Glory Church!

The Lord's Glory Church is a Spirit-filled church that holds the Bible as the only infallible and authoritative written Word of God. We believe in the Holy Trinity; the deity of our Lord Jesus Christ; salvation by grace, apart from works, through faith in the Lord Jesus Christ; the new birth; the baptism in the Holy Spirit; water baptism by immersion; and the gifts of the Holy Spirit as being viable and applicable to the church today.

Our motto is "Real Love, Real People."
Our vision is "To find purpose in life through loving God and loving people."

Contact Information
The Lord's Glory Church
461 Artesian Plaza Drive, Humble, TX 77338
Telephone: 281-446-0091
E-mail: info@glorychurch.com

For Service Times and Directions visit us online!

Website: www.glorychurch.com
Facebook: www.facebook.com/thelordsglory
Twitter: @thelordsglory
Instagram: thelordsglory

All services can also be viewed LIVE at www.glorychurch.com/live or Facebook Live or YouTube.

Made in the USA
Coppell, TX
19 April 2022

76787289R00081